The Dawn of Man

The Dawn of Man

Illustrated by Zdeněk Burian

Text by Josef Wolf

Edited and adapted by
Peter Andrews · Robin Harvey
Colin Ridler · Christopher Stringer

Harry N. Abrams, Inc., Publishers, New York

Frontispiece: Java man — artist's reconstruction based on
the skull found at Trinil by Eugene Dubois in 1891 — 2.

Library of Congress Catalogue Card
Number: 77-93512
International Standard Book Number:
0-8109-0810-7

Pradějiny člověka copyright © 1978
Artia, Prague
English edition copyright © 1978
Thames and Hudson, Ltd., London
and Artia, Prague
Published in 1978 by Harry N. Abrams,
Incorporated, New York

Translated by Margot Schierlová
Graphic design by Aleš Krejča

Printed and bound in Czechoslovakia
3/99/30/51-01

Contents

PONGO
PYGMAEUS

GORILLA
GORILLA

PAN
TROGLODYTES

HOMO SAPIENS
SAPIENS

HOMO SAPIENS
NEANDERTHALENSIS

HOMO
SAPIENS
RHODESIEN

PARANTHROPUS
ROBUSTUS

HOMO SAPIENS
STEINHEIMENSIS

HOMO
ERECTUS
PEKINENSIS

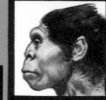

GIGANTOPITHECUS

AUSTRALOPITHECUS
AFRICANUS

HOMO ERECTUS
ERECTUS

HOMO
HABILIS

RAMAPITHECUS

OREOPITHECUS

PROCONSUL

ANCESTRAL
DRYOPITHECINE

1 The successful ape

The history of human society, as defined by the keeping of written records, began in ancient Egypt, in Mesopotamia, in India, and in China, at approximately the same time, about 3000 BC. The end of prehistoric times did not come at the same time everywhere, however, and relics of these conditions still exist in a number of isolated and particularly backward regions. For instance, some of the original inhabitants of Australia, the aborigines, still live at Stone Age level in the bush on the edges of the deserts, just as their forebears did long ago. The same applies to the last descendants of the Bushmen and pygmies of Africa and to the Semangs, Sukais and other groups of negritos on the Malayan peninsula and in other parts of Asia.

How has man changed, and what has been his physical and mental evolution during the past three million years? How did he come to originate at all and where did the different evolutionary types and species in the various phases of his prehistory come from? Who is man and what are the cultures and human society to which we want to give most of our attention in this book?

Man is a highly developed living being, but he is also an inseparable part of nature and of the animal world. He is likewise largely dependent on nature; for example, his growth, development and ageing follow biological laws and he lives on both vegetable and animal food. Physically, man has many features and attributes similar, even identical, to those of other animals. Among extant animals, the anthropoid apes (the chimpanzee, gorilla and orang-utan) resemble man the most closely in their anatomy. We cannot regard them as near relatives, but they are at least the closest we have and are something like second cousins. Man is tied by a looser bond of kinship to the other primates (the lemurs, lorises and tarsiers).

On the other hand, man differs from all other animals in many respects, such as his permanently erect posture, the size and function of his brain, and his mode of life in societies. He is also the only living creature capable of conscious action, of working and producing and of actively controlling nature itself for a useful purpose. Thus although the human species is unquestionably a natural species, since it is dependent on natural conditions for survival of the individual, persistence of the race, and the maintenance of life, man's ability to create a secondary environment through his culture has separated him from other animals. Primitive man evolved into social, cultural and civilized man as he altered his conditions and himself by continuous, purposeful and consciously directed activity; this eventually led to the highest forms of science and art, culture and civilization.

Our place in nature

Man's classification in the natural system is evidence of his animal origin and his kinship with the rest of the animal kingdom:
PHYLUM Chordata (chordates)
 SUBPHYLUM Vertebrata (vertebrates)
  CLASS Mammalia (mammals)
   SUBCLASS Eutheria (placental mammals)
   ORDER Primates
    SUBORDER Anthropoidea (higher primates)
     SUPERFAMILY Hominoidea (hominoids)
     FAMILY Hominidae (hominids)
      GENUS *Homo* (man)
       SPECIES *Homo sapiens* (intelligent man)
        SUBSPECIES *Homo sapiens sapiens* (modern intelligent man)

The evolution of the higher primates from a common ancestral stock: the apes (Pongidae) on the left branch, and man and his forerunners (Hominidae) on the right.

The order Primates is divided into two, the Prosimii and the Anthropoidea. The prosimians are lemurs, lorises and tarsiers which are mostly nocturnal and live in tropical Africa and Asia. Little is known of the recent history of these animals but they are very common in the fossil record in deposits ranging from 40 to 60 million years old. The anthropoid group consists of the Old World and New World monkeys, the apes of Africa and Asia — and man. They have a mainly tropical distribution but are also found in warm temperate regions, and by contrast with the prosimians they are active during the day.

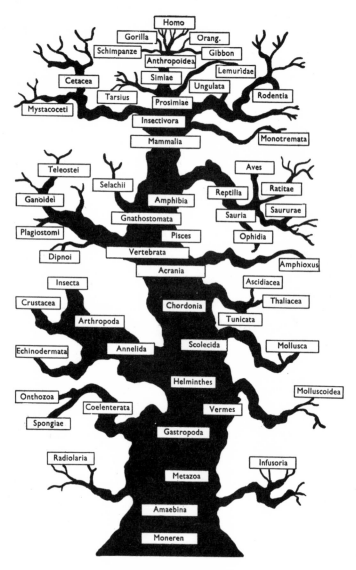

Ernst Haeckel, contemporary and supporter of Charles Darwin, devised this 'family tree' to illustrate the evolution of all living things. Man, flanked by the apes, is at the top of the tree.

The anthropoids first appeared in the fossil record about 25 to 35 million years ago, but they spread rapidly and displaced the prosimians from most of their habitats. Today the remaining prosimians form relic populations and they have reduced potential competition with the higher primates by being small nocturnal insect-eating animals. The apes, from which man is an offshoot, are also relic populations today, although they were the first of the groups of higher primates to diversify and replace the prosimians. The monkeys in their turn have displaced the apes and taken over much of their former range. It can be said, therefore, that man comes from one of the less successful primate groups, a group that flourished 10 to 30 million years ago, but which is now in danger of extinction. Man's origin in the group is towards the end of this period and it is possible that his evolution represents one of the ways in which the apes were forced to adapt to compete with the more successful monkeys.

Likenesses and differences

The anatomical structure of the anthropoid apes is very similar to that of man. They have basically similar bones, muscles and teeth, and their soft anatomy is practically identical. They have a similarly constructed brain: the brain of the chimpanzee, for example, differs from the brain of monkeys more than it does from the human brain. The body of an anthropoid ape is covered not with fur (the woolly part is missing), but only with long hair. Anthropoid apes are likewise subject to many of the same diseases as man, mainly owing to the similar structure of their internal organs and their functions and to the presence of some of the same blood groups. At least two of the human blood groups occur in anthropoid apes.

Man's typical features and most striking characteristics originate during the embryonic stages of his development. Here again we find numerous points of similarity with anthropoid apes. At birth, the brain of an infant gorilla is almost as large as the brain of a human infant (about 350 cc), but after birth the gorilla's brain grows very slowly, while a child's brain grows very fast during the first years of life. Later on, it slows down, but it does not stop growing until the child becomes adult.

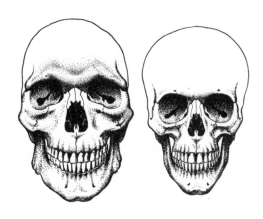

Characteristic differences between the skulls of a modern human male (left) *and a female. Note the much greater robustness of the male skull.*

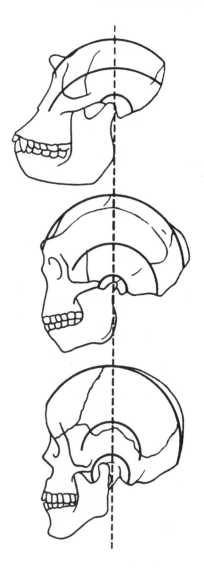

The architecture of the skull. Top to bottom: *gorilla, primitive man,* Homo sapiens. *They are connected by a line passing through the ears, which demonstrates how, in man, the cranium is expanded relatively to the face, while in the gorilla the face projects further forward from the line.*

Another fact which testifies to the relationship of man and the anthropoid apes is that certain structures and attributes which persist or continue to develop in man actually appear for a time in the embryos of anthropoid apes. One of these is the distribution of the hair in man and the chimpanzee. The hair of a seven-month chimpanzee embryo is distributed in exactly the same way as that of a new-born human infant: we find the same fine, long hair on the head and the same smooth skin covered on the body with short, almost invisible downy hair. The chimpanzee later has dark-coloured skin, but prior to birth it is very pale grey, tinged with pink.

We could quote from embryology a whole series of further details on the evolutionary associations between man and the anthropoid apes. The human embryo develops in exactly the same way as other animals. The earliest stages resemble each other the most closely and the successive appearance of human characters begins later. Comparative physiology likewise furnishes a wealth of evidence on the function of the various organs of the same individual and the organs of different groups of animals. For instance, human bones have almost the same composition as the bones of other higher vertebrates, while human blood plasma has approximately the same mineral salts content as the plasma of other mammals (that is why some important vaccines can be prepared from the serum of certain animals).

If man is so similar to the great apes we have next to ask, in what way is he different? The main anatomical features differentiating man from all other animals are as follows:

1   In man the cranial part of the head is larger than the facial part, and the high braincase forms a bulging forehead. The arch of the jaw is short and horseshoe-shaped, and has no spaces for the canines; the canines are incisor-like, they do not project beyond the other teeth, and they display only small sex-related size differences. The premolars are 'grinding' teeth, and the third premolar particularly has lost any trace of its primitive cutting function. The eyes are capable of both black-and-white and colour vision. The outer part of the ear terminates in a lobe and has a curled rim. The nasal bones project

9

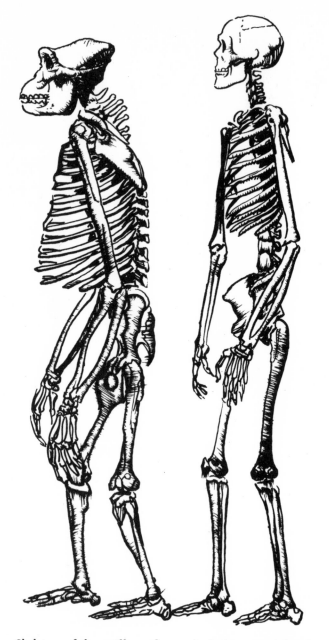

from the face and are fitted together like a roof. Only *Homo sapiens sapiens* has a noticeably jutting chin. The mucous membrane covers the outside of the lips to a considerable distance and the upper lip has a groove in the centre.

2 The human brain is several times larger than that of anthropoid apes and in relation to body weight it is heavier. The formation of a large number of convolutions has increased the surface of the brain to about two square metres; and the structure of the brain tissue is also more complex.

3 The spine has two S-shaped bends, an adaptation to upright posture.

4 The pelvis is wide and carries the whole weight of the trunk, distributing the pressure on the lower limbs.

5 The arms are mobile and they lack the weight-bearing specialization present in the great apes. The freeing of the arms from their locomotor function makes them available for other uses, initially probably food gathering and carrying, but later the full range of man's activities. The human hand has a well-developed thumb, very large relative to the fingers, and the hand is adapted for high-precision gripping of objects.

6 The legs are very long in relation to the trunk and are adapted for bearing the full body weight. The foot has longitudinal and lateral arches for softening the impact on the ground. Much of the stress during walking is taken through the big toe, which in man is not divergent but is parallel to the other toes. It is also by far the most robust of the five toes.

Skeletons of the gorilla and man, both shown upright. Note the differences in the position of the skull on the spine, and the curvature of the spine, also the gorilla's longer arms and the longer legs in man.

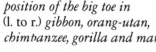

Structure of the foot and position of the big toe in (l. to r.) gibbon, orang-utan, chimpanzee, gorilla and man.

Brain power

This list can be summarized into two major characters that are unique to man: his large skull and brain size, with all its related features, and the fact that he walks upright on two legs. During man's evolution, his brain can be seen to have undergone great change. At the stage when the evolutionary line of the primitive anthropoids divided into one branch leading to the present-day anthropoid apes and another leading to man, the brain probably had a capacity of about 250—350 cc. In those remote ancestors of man called the australopithecines it was already 428—530 cc. The brain of *Homo erectus* (1,000—1,250 cc) was three times the size of the chimpanzee's brain (410 cc) and the brain of modern man is still larger. Growth and development of the human brain must have been accompanied by increasing complexity and variety of communication. For much of the early history of man this would have been limited to chimpanzee-like sounds and gestures, and it may not have been until *Homo sapiens sapiens* emerged during the past 40,000 years that speech developed more rapidly and primitive languages were formed.

Man's exceptional position in nature and the differences between man and animals are also due to other developments of the human brain. Man does not see better than birds and there are many species which surpass him in swiftness, strength, hearing and a sense of smell. Unlike animals, however, man can live in any climate and any surroundings, he can penetrate the Earth's depths, climb the highest mountains and venture out into space; he has mastered the use of fire and has learnt all about the atom and how to control it — all as a result of the development of his brain and the use of his hands.

Since man first came into existence, his most significant and most important activity has been work, i.e. activity with a specific aim, a thing which does not exist among animals. Work is the true prerogative of the human race and it indubitably played the main role in man's evolution. Most animal activities are instinctive (though some can be learned), but only man consciously alters his work to suit his requirements and at the same time alters his physical and mental activity and makes himself master of his environment. Animals influence nature simply by existing in it, for instance by moving about in it and living on its produce, but man, through his work, has

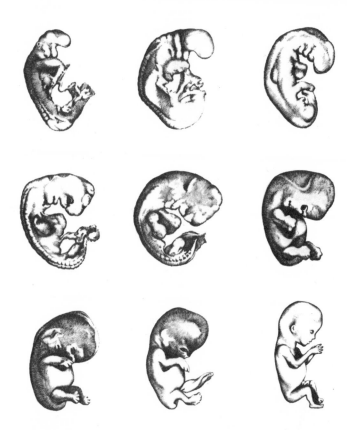

Individual stages in the development of the human embryo. To begin with, it closely resembles the developing embryo of other animals, and only gradually do human features and organs emerge.

a much greater effect on nature and leaves traces of his activities behind him. When animals die out, nature remains basically unchanged, whereas every human generation leaves behind it concrete reminders of its working activity.

Man, the tool-maker

One of the first expressions of human activity, that is work, is the stone tools manufactured by man during the earliest part of the Palaeolithic period by breaking up natural pebbles. The resultant stone-cores and flakes, at first, were of a random and indeterminate shape; the waste flakes produced in making them were also themselves used without any additional working. These tools have been found associated with several different types of early man and it is not known which one actually made them; the Olduvai

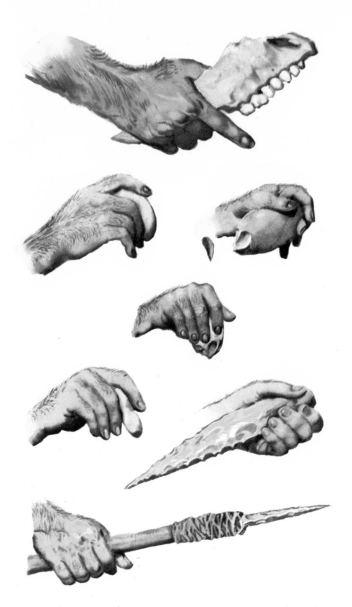

Gorge in Tanzania is one of the best-known sites where they have been found. Crude pebble tools of this kind were later worked, by chipping on two faces, into characteristically shaped hand-axes and cleavers. These, which were much more efficient tools, were first developed in Africa, where they have been found in association with the ape-man *Homo erectus;* he lived in Java and parts of China as well as Africa, but only the African branch had developed the more sophisticated form of tool. Later on, man evolved better production techniques, allowing the shape and size of the flakes to be determined beforehand. The surface of a natural pebble was first of all 'peeled' (crudely shaped) and a perpendicular striking surface was chipped off on one of the apices of the egg-shaped core; a vertical blow was then aimed at the surface and a blade with a definite form was flaked off. This was then shaped by secondary flaking into a variety of forms, making scrapers, knives and points.

Late in the Pleistocene, around 200,000 years ago, lived what are generally held to be the first representatives of our own species, *Homo sapiens.*

The oldest ways of producing and using tools. Top to bottom: *using bone as a weapon or tool; use of crude pebbles in the so-called 'pebble industry'; production of stone flakes and points; hafting the stone tool to a wooden handle.*

Reconstruction of a method of flint working during the late Palaeolithic. Holding the flint firm under the punch with a protected left knee is a conjecture, derived from American Indians.

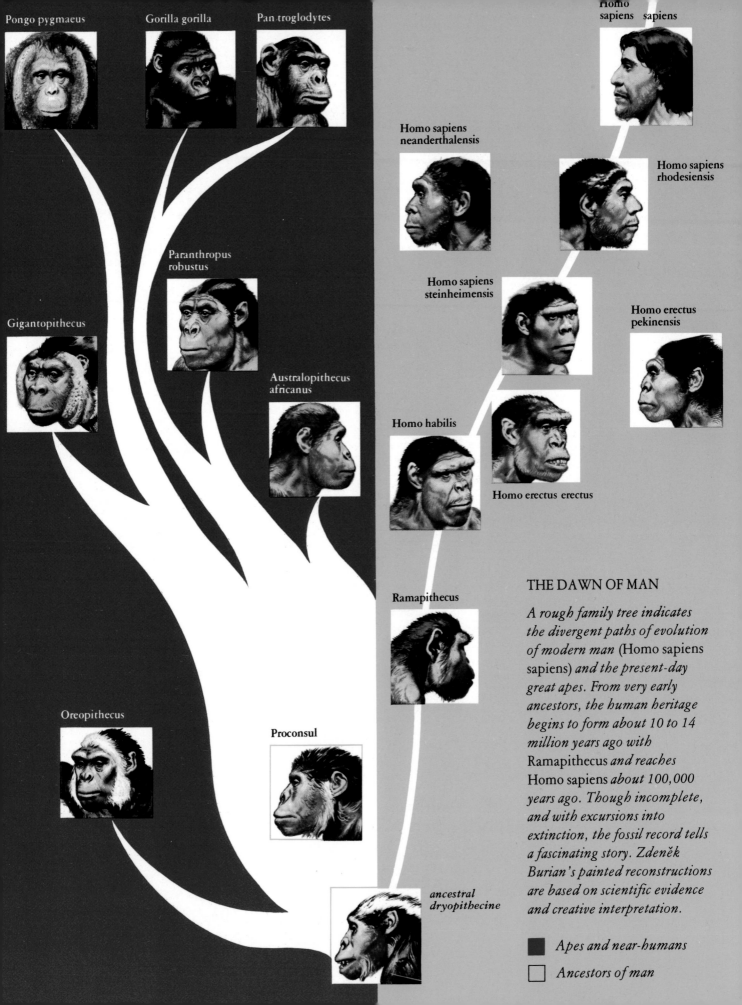

Pongo pygmaeus

Gorilla gorilla

Pan troglodytes

Homo sapiens sapiens

Homo sapiens neanderthalensis

Homo sapiens rhodesiensis

Paranthropus robustus

Homo sapiens steinheimensis

Homo erectus pekinensis

Gigantopithecus

Australopithecus africanus

Homo habilis

Homo erectus erectus

Ramapithecus

Oreopithecus

Proconsul

ancestral dryopithecine

THE DAWN OF MAN

A rough family tree indicates the divergent paths of evolution of modern man (Homo sapiens sapiens) *and the present-day great apes. From very early ancestors, the human heritage begins to form about 10 to 14 million years ago with* Ramapithecus *and reaches* Homo sapiens *about 100,000 years ago. Though incomplete, and with excursions into extinction, the fossil record tells a fascinating story. Zdeněk Burian's painted reconstructions are based on scientific evidence and creative interpretation.*

■ *Apes and near-humans*

□ *Ancestors of man*

Named Neanderthal man *(Homo sapiens neanderthalensis)* from the first discovered specimen in the Neander valley, Germany, they inhabited large parts of Europe, the Middle East and North Africa. Frequently found associated with Neanderthal man is the stone industry called Mousterian (after the site of Le Moustier in France). Mousterian tools were made from rather large flakes which were sharpened and shaped by fine secondary flaking. The main implements were scrapers, that is a broad blade retouched along one side and used probably for skinning and cutting up animals. Other implements included leaf-like points, broad wedges and points. The Mousterian industry is not always associated with Neanderthal man, however, and in some cases Neanderthal man has been found associated with hand-axe industries, so that even in this case there does not seem to be a direct relation between the primitive hominid* and his stone industry.

When *Homo sapiens sapiens* first appeared in the Middle East about 34,000 years ago, a new technique of tool-working appeared, characterized by long, thin blades struck from prepared cores and then fashioned into many different shapes and sizes of blade, leaf-shaped spear points, awls, scrapers, and several others. Many different forms of blade tools are known, often superimposed in individual caves which indicates migrations and the replacement of one group of Upper Palaeolithic man by another; but all are essentially similar and all are associated with modern man. There are some cases where Upper Palaeolithic industries follow a Mousterian industry, and in these cases it appears possible that modern man replaced Neanderthal in that particular region.

Stone tools represent the most readily preservable evidence of man's early activity, but at all stages of man's evolution there is little doubt that other material was also used. Stone tools would have been supplemented by bone and wooden ones, represented mainly by cleavers, spearheads, awls, bodkins, crude hammers, clubs and hammer-stones, and later also by finer tools like needles and hooks, which made it possible to manufacture objects such as necklaces made of bone beads, rings of mammoth ivory, drilled

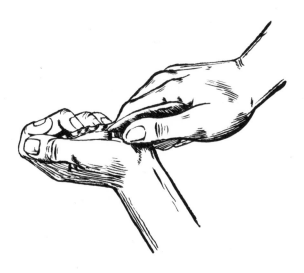

One method—called 'pressure flaking'—of sharpening a stone tool after it has been roughly hammered into shape.

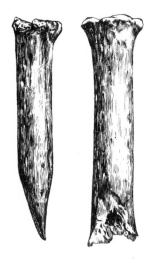

The very early development of tools. Top row: *bones needed practically no working.* Middle row: *pebbles, with a minimum of working, made hand-held hammers. These would serve to chip lumps of flint* (bottom row) *to make the first edged tools.*

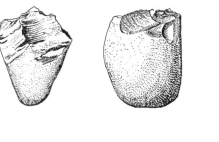

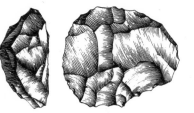

* Any member of the family Hominidae (see p. 7); this includes both modern man and his fossil ancestors.

13

shells and animals' teeth (bear, reindeer, wolf and boar).

In the last phases of the prehistory of human society, in the Mesolithic and Neolithic periods, prehistoric *Homo sapiens* improved his stone-working techniques to such a degree that he was able to produce the finest stone tools, sharpened, polished and bored, such as axes, hammers, knives and a variety of points, sickles and files. In the latest Stone Age, he produced them alongside the first crude copper and bronze, and eventually iron, implements, until the metals finally superseded stone. Stone, bone and wooden tools still continued to be produced and used for special purposes, such as millstones for crushing grain, and wooden wheels, hafts and handles. Stone was relegated more and more to the role of building material, which was used for the most varied purposes, from the building of gravestones and barrows to the construction of grandiose religious cult monuments like Stonehenge.

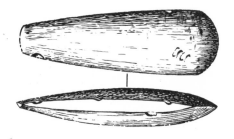

The Neolithic period ('New Stone Age') saw the highest development of tool-making in stone. The chopper (above) *and axe shown here were carefully and expertly shaped, and finished off by grinding the stone surface smooth.*

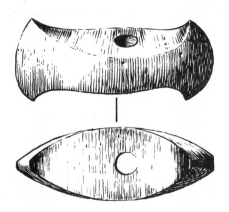

Survey of geological eras and periods

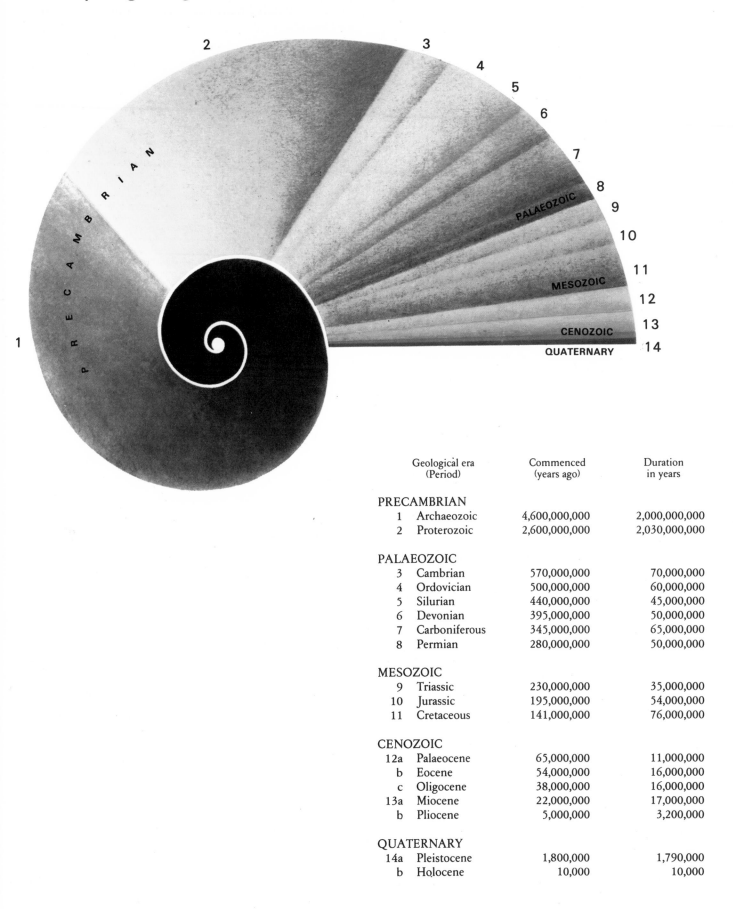

Geological era (Period)		Commenced (years ago)	Duration in years
PRECAMBRIAN			
1	Archaeozoic	4,600,000,000	2,000,000,000
2	Proterozoic	2,600,000,000	2,030,000,000
PALAEOZOIC			
3	Cambrian	570,000,000	70,000,000
4	Ordovician	500,000,000	60,000,000
5	Silurian	440,000,000	45,000,000
6	Devonian	395,000,000	50,000,000
7	Carboniferous	345,000,000	65,000,000
8	Permian	280,000,000	50,000,000
MESOZOIC			
9	Triassic	230,000,000	35,000,000
10	Jurassic	195,000,000	54,000,000
11	Cretaceous	141,000,000	76,000,000
CENOZOIC			
12a	Palaeocene	65,000,000	11,000,000
b	Eocene	54,000,000	16,000,000
c	Oligocene	38,000,000	16,000,000
13a	Miocene	22,000,000	17,000,000
b	Pliocene	5,000,000	3,200,000
QUATERNARY			
14a	Pleistocene	1,800,000	1,790,000
b	Holocene	10,000	10,000

2 The world before man

Our planet is nearly 5,000 million years old. Little is known of its early history, but a great part of its cosmic age must have been taken up by its progressive conversion from inanimate stellar material to the Earth which gave rise to life.

Evidence has been found to show that life on the Earth dates back to the Archaeozoic ('ancient life') or early Precambrian (see p. 15). This lasted about two thousand million years (from 4.6 to 2.6 thousand million years ago), and during this time the Earth's crust was formed. Abundant and violent volcanic activity veiled it in steamy fumes and gases, from which flames of incandescent magma shot up from time to time from the centre of the Earth. When these rock-forming processes on the Earth's surface had died down, the atmosphere and the seas were formed, heralding a further important chapter in the Earth's prehistory. The rays of the sun were now better able to penetrate right to the solid surface of the planet, where their life-giving energy contributed to the birth of life. The most satisfactory medium for the appearance of the first microscopic living creatures seems to have been the warm, shallow lagoons on the shores of the primeval oceans and the near-shore lava reefs which were continuously washed by their warm water.

The first living micro-organisms were not yet differentiated into plants and animals. Even today, bacteria, viruses and other micro-organisms still form a specific and relatively separate world, with its own evolution and its own mode of life, different from that of more highly organized plants and animals. It was from these undifferentiated but living particles of matter that the first plant and animal

The Earth's surface in the Precambrian, 3,000 million years ago, at a time when the first living micro-organisms appeared, nurtured in the warm, salt-rich waters of the primeval seas by the action of the sun's rays.

micro-organisms evolved, to lay the foundations of the vegetable and animal kingdoms.

According to modern research, life on the Earth originated about one thousand million years after the Earth itself was formed, i.e. about 3.5 to 3.3 thousand million years ago. The evolution of life continued during the middle and late Precambrian, from 2,600 to 570 million years ago. Rare finds of Precambrian fossils show imprints of the single-celled bodies of microscopic organisms which were probably alga-like organisms and evolved as the first representatives of the vegetable kingdom. They apparently covered the offshore reefs like huge, irregular carpets and spread over the Earth's surface anywhere where they found sufficient water and warmth. These living carpets were at first probably only different shades of green and blue-green, since their cells were able to produce only small chlorophyll granules. Later, when multicellular types of algae evolved, the Earth could have been covered with other colours, yellow, orange and reddish brown, as well as with green and blue-green algae. The very fact that these primitive plant organisms, using the sun's energy, were able to manufacture complex organic substances from carbon dioxide and water and to live, reproduce and nourish their vast progeny, shows how fundamentally important they were for the further evolution of life on the Earth.

The first living things

The oldest forms of animal life on the Earth were also single-celled organisms. Later, various multicellular marine organisms appeared, which either lived freely in the great seas, or led a stationary existence on their shores or bed. Animals probably started to evolve later than plants, but from the outset their evolution progressed very quickly in different directions. In the

The Palaeozoic era saw the first land animals and plants, some 300 million years ago. Reconstructed here from fossil remains are centipedes, a four-footed amphibian, Solenodonsaurus *('pipe-toothed lizard') and the giant dragonfly* Meganeura, *with a thirty-inch wing span.*

The Mesozoic era, about 200 million years ago, saw the evolution of many new kinds of reptiles on land, some of huge size. Here are Scutosaurus *('shield lizard') and the sabre-toothed predator* Sauroctonus *('lizard-killer').*

latest Precambrian, the Earth was already inhabited by animals which resembled marine worms, by the first precursors of brachiopods (lampshells), echinoderms (such as starfish and sea urchins) and of primitive crustaceans, and by the oldest known predecessor of the arthropods, or segmented animals, called *Protadelaidea* after the town of Adelaide in South Australia near which it was found.

When the Earth was about four thousand million years old, that is some one thousand million years ago, plants and animals embarked on a period of tremendous expansion, which led eventually to the evolution of man. Man's birth and evolution were preceded, however, by long epochs in which many thousands of generations of weird and wonderful creatures appeared on the Earth, only to perish again after a time. Man had to wait for over 500 million years before conditions were ripe for him to take the stage. As one of the most recent evolutionary experiments, man appeared only a few seconds before the Earth's geological clock struck 12, but the origin

and evolution of the human race may eventually become the culminating point of the whole process of world genesis.

The age of the fishes

Some 570 million years ago, an era known as the Primary or Palaeozoic ('old life'), began in the evolution of life on the Earth. Since life at the beginning of this geological era was concentrated in the seas and numerous new forms of marine life evolved, the Palaeozoic era in general, and the Devonian period in particular, are known as the age of the fishes. In the animal zoological system, fishes are the lowest group of vertebrates and it was from them that all the other groups, including mammals, evolved.

In the earliest geological period of the Palaeozoic era (the Cambrian), some 570 to 500 million years ago, organisms with a lime-based skeleton in their

body began to flourish. At the end of this period, primitive forms of crustaceans, the trilobites, appeared. At the same time the first representatives of the Chordata, animals whose body was reinforced by a primitive axial skeleton *(chorda dorsalis)* also appeared. In some marine animals this skeleton remained simple and compact, while in others it developed into a bony spine composed of separate vertebrae. This characteristic feature of the vertebrates can be traced throughout animal evolution from the first fishes.

The oldest groups of fishes probably had only a *chorda dorsalis,* but no jaws or teeth. Instead of a mouth they had a simple sucker-like opening and were therefore known as 'jawless' fish (Agnatha). They were evidently related to the still extant lampreys. The first of them appeared during the Ordovician period, 500 to 440 million years ago.

The first bony fishes, together with the first terrestrial animals and plants, date back to the next two periods of the Palaeozoic era — the Silurian

period (440—395 million years ago) and the Devonian period (395—345 million years ago). Lung fishes (Dipnoi) and fringe-finned fishes (Crossopterygia) originated at this time. A few representatives of these last two groups still inhabit warm salt and fresh water in the southern hemisphere (e. g. the coelacanth), as genuine 'living fossils'. Other groups of marine creatures died out altogether, however, leaving no successors at all.

The first reptiles

If the early Palaeozoic era (the Cambrian, Ordovician, Silurian and Devonian periods) was characterized by rapid evolution of fishes and the first dry-land plants and animals, the later part, starting with the Carboniferous period (345—280 million years ago) and culminating in the Permian period (280—230 million years ago), can be described as the age of amphibians and the first reptiles. One of the very first

Reptiles grew larger and larger, until they reached the end of the evolutionary line in the Jurassic, 150 million years ago, *with 50-ton, 90-foot monsters like* Diplodocus. *For animals as large as this, there is no way but out.*

four-legged animals to inhabit the dry land was probably the primitive amphibian *Ichthyostega,* which evolved from early forms of fringe-finned fishes, such as the Devonian *Eusthenopteron.* The fossilized bones of *Ichthyostega* have been found in upper Devonian layers in Greenland. The Carboniferous period was the time of the greatest expansion of amphibians. Later on during this period, some of their more advanced forms gave rise to the first mammal-like reptiles, from which the first primitive mammals evolved during the Triassic period (230—195 million years ago).

By the end of the Palaeozoic era, life flourished almost everywhere in the seas and in fresh water and was expanding equally on the dry land. The development of the Carboniferous forests and abundant green flora favoured the evolution of the amphibians, reptiles, molluscs and insects. Numerous

species of aquatic worms, corals, sponges, trilobites and insect larvae supplemented the diverse fish population, in which, at the end of the Palaeozoic era, giant armoured fishes like *Dinichthys* and primitive sharks of the genus *Xenacanthus* predominated. Great dragonflies of the genus *Meganeura,* with a wingspan of about 75 cm, darted about by the waterside, while the Carboniferous and Permian swamps were inhabited by large numbers of amphibians with the most varied forms, from the serpentine *Dolichosoma longissimum* to agile four-legged types like *Urocordylus* and *Diplovertebron.*

During the Carboniferous period, the first reptiles — the lizard-like saurians — made their appearance at the margin of the forests of horsetails and among the ancient tree-like club-mosses. During the Permian period, the dry land and the water were still inhabited by many diverse species of small and large plant-eating and carnivorous saurians, such as *Mesosaurus,* whose bones have been found in South Africa and Brazil. Reptiles first of all evolved as terrestrial animals, whose bodies were covered with scales and, in some cases, armour plating, and only later did aquatic forms evolve from the terrestrial ones. The expansion of reptiles at the end of the Palaeozoic era was also stimulated by the geological and climatic conditions on the Earth. The marginal seas dried up, the amount of dry land increased and deserts and semi-deserts were actually formed in places. Many ancient types of plants became extinct and many types of aquatic animals died out. Intensive oxidation took place on the surface of Permian layers, staining the rocks red and reddish brown. This striking period marked the beginning of a further era in the Earth's geological history, the Mesozoic or Secondary era.

New forms of life

The change in climatic conditions at the end of the Palaeozoic and the beginning of the Mesozoic era led to the evolution of new and quite different forms of plants and animals. The disappearance of the Carboniferous forests, together with their fish- and amphibian-filled swamps, opened up new possibilities for reptiles preferring dry land. Almost the whole of the Mesozoic era (230—65 million years ago) was characterized by the successive evolution of new species of reptiles — saurians, dinosaurs, pterosaurs and ichthyosaurs — most of whose highly specialized and giant forms died out during further natural and climatic changes.

The Mesozoic era was a period of widespread proliferation of gymnospermous plants (plants whose seeds are unprotected by seed vessels), the most characteristic of which were cycads and conifers; among the latter, giant sequoias and cypresses were dominant by the end of the era. Green horsetails and club-mosses still grew in some parts of the world, especially where the ground was still moist, but they were much smaller and their numbers were limited. The great stretches of desert and semi-desert country gave way only slowly before the new plants, conspicuous for the bizarre shapes of cycads and gingkos.

The Triassic, the first period of the Mesozoic era

(230—195 million years ago), saw further marked differentiation of animal life. Different new forms of the spirally coiled shellfish called ammonites appeared in the oceans, until they eventually dominated the seas and river beds. On the dry land, reptiles continued to expand at the expense of practically all other terrestrial animals. During the Triassic, and even more during the Jurassic period, plant-eating and carnivorous saurians attaining a length of 30 metres and over, and weighing up to 10 tons, supplanted the majority of amphibians and small reptiles. Almost all the species of mammal-like reptiles, the probable precursors of mammals, were also mere outsiders on the fringe of animal societies. During the Triassic period a few new species appeared among them; and although few, they were very important for evolution since it was from them that the first mammals evolved.

Interesting evolutionary changes took place in these mammalian precursors. Their jaws, which were originally composed of several bones, fused to form a single bone. Their skulls developed a depression at the temple and they acquired an inner ear, an entirely

One of the earliest ancestors of the mammals, Triconodon, *could perhaps be called 'a reptile with hair'. From fossil teeth and jaws, it is considered to have been carnivorous, and though it probably laid eggs it may have suckled its young—the definition of a mammal.*

new organ of hearing; their once conical teeth were differentiated to several types until in time they acquired the mammalian form of dentition with complex cusps.

Small mammal-like reptiles living right at the end of the Triassic period were the ancestors of the small, mouse-sized mammal *Triconodon,* one of the most primitive forms of Jurassic mammals. It probably still laid eggs like a reptile, but its body was covered with simple fur and it lived on small animals, like its older relatives from the South African Triassic.

The next Mesozoic period, the Jurassic (195—141 million years ago), is famed for the appearance of the first birds, which evolved from other transitory reptile forms. *Archaeopteryx* ('ancient wing'), the oldest primitive bird, still had jaws with teeth in them, but its forelimbs had been transformed to wings covered with feathers. More advanced forms of primitive birds, represented by the genera *Ichthyornis* ('fish

bird') and *Hesperornis* ('western bird'), date back to the last period of the Mesozoic era, the Cretaceous (141—65 million years ago).

During this time, the evolution of mammals led to the appearance of further new groups. At the end of the Cretaceous period they were differentiated to pouched mammals (Metatheria) and placental mammals (Eutheria), i.e. true mammals with a placenta. These early mammals lived during the Jurassic and Cretaceous periods alongside the giant saurians; for instance skeletons of one of the biggest dinosaurs, *Diplodocus carnegii,* have been found in Jurassic strata in Wyoming, Utah and Colorado, and one has recently been reported from England. At the end of the Cretaceous period, when most of the Mesozoic dry-land reptiles had died out, a remarkable expansion of mammals culminated in the appearance of many of the extant eutherian Orders, including the insect-eaters and the first primates.

A Miocene landscape, 20 million years ago. By now, plant and animal life looks more like what we know today—the flamingo-like Palaelodus, *the elephantine mastodon, the deer* Dicrocerus *(with antlers) and* Palaeomeryx.

The age of the mammals

Mammals quickly became widespread at the beginning of the last geological era, the Cenozoic era. This lasted about 65 million years, and during this time both land and sea were dominated by mammals, with the evolution of practically all their known forms. For this reason the Cenozoic era is known as the age of mammals. In fact, however, the Cenozoic era was also the age of birds, and even more so of plants, especially angiosperms (plants whose seeds are protected by a seed-case).

At first, conifers such as *Chamaecyparis* and *Taxodium* were common in the warm, swampy Tertiary forests, but most of them later died out and their partly preserved remains formed extensive lignite (soft coal) deposits. For the most part deciduous forests predominated in the early part of the Cenozoic era (the Palaeocene, Eocene and Oligocene periods), 65 — 22 million years ago, when there was a warm subtropical climate in the north of Europe and America. Climates were also warm in the present subtropical belt, and magnolias, forsythias and other plants which liked warmth grew equally well in Greece and in Spitzbergen.

In the next part of the Cenozoic era, the Miocene and Pliocene periods, conditions underwent a striking change. The warmth-loving flora and fauna retreated towards the equator and their place in the northern hemisphere was taken by forests composed of oak, ash, beech, elm and other deciduous trees and of conifers and flowering plants like the ones we know today.

The fauna of the more recent Cenozoic, especially the Miocene (22 — 5 million years ago), included mastodons, and primitive hoofed creatures (ungulates) of the genera *Palaeomeryx* and *Dicrocerus* (with antlers). During this time the horse also evolved from a small, fox-like, five-toed ancestor to a one-toed ungulate by the end of the Cenozoic era. Among the many bird species, the most striking were giant flightless birds, and flamingos of the genus *Palaelodus,* which mainly inhabited Europe.

The first undisputed representatives of early man—australopithecines, whose fossil remains have been found in Africa dating from 3 to 1 million years ago.

Monkeys, apes and man

The most important forms of Cenozoic animals from the point of view of human evolution were undoubtedly the primates, which originated from a group of very small, primitive insect-eaters. The earliest primates are classified as prosimians (see p. 27), and during the Palaeocene they displayed great variety of adaptation in the shift from insectivorous to herbivorous diets. Most of these experimental lines died out in the Palaeocene, and by the Eocene the main subdivisions of present-day primates were distinguished. The first of the higher primates, or Anthropoidea, are known from the Oligocene, and these proliferated in the Miocene to produce the monkeys, apes and man. The New World monkeys probably had a prosimian origin independently from the Old World monkeys and apes, but little is known of this. The differentiation into monkeys (with tails) and apes (tailless) appears to have taken place in the earliest Miocene, but for much of this period monkeys were uncommon and the primate fauna was dominated by the apes. This position is reversed at the present time, and now monkeys are more successful than the apes.

23

In the later part of the Miocene one line of apes moved out of the tropical forest zone to which they had previously been limited and occupied the widespread woodlands of more northerly latitudes. From them the earliest hominids evolved and by the Pliocene they had developed into the first undisputed representatives of early man. These are called australopithecines ('southern apes'), and from them the first members of the genus *Homo* emerged at the beginning of the Quaternary era.

The Quaternary era, which has lasted about two million years, has been a further important stage in the evolution of plants and animals on the Earth. It has been marked by a succession of glacial periods and interglacials with numerous natural and climatic changes, and by the migration, death and extinction of various species of animals and plants. It was precisely under these variable conditions that the hominids evolved and progressed. While highly specialized species like the mammoth, the woolly rhinoceros, the sabre-tooth tiger, the cave bear and others were dying out, the hominids, less specialized in form and structure, evolved faster than ever before.

In three million years, the genus *Homo* passed through three successive stages of evolution, each characterized by a new species — *Homo habilis* ('handy man'), *Homo erectus* ('upright man'), and *Homo sapiens* ('intelligent man'). *Homo sapiens* formed two distinct subspecies during his evolution — *Homo sapiens neanderthalensis* and *Homo sapiens sapiens*. The evolution of the genus *Homo* at first took place far to the south of the ice barrier, in regions rich in vegetation and animal life in the tropical and subtropical belt of Africa, Asia and Europe, and only gradually did our forerunners spread further north. It was not until much later that conditions became favourable for man's general spread, so that he rapidly populated the rest of the Earth and steadily increased in numbers.

The Quaternary era is not yet over. It has continued into historic times and will probably last for further thousands or millions of years, as long as man and human cultures and societies still exist. The genesis of the Earth, culminating in the genesis of man, is not finished, but will continue with the further evolution of plants, animals and man himself.

The evolution of all living things

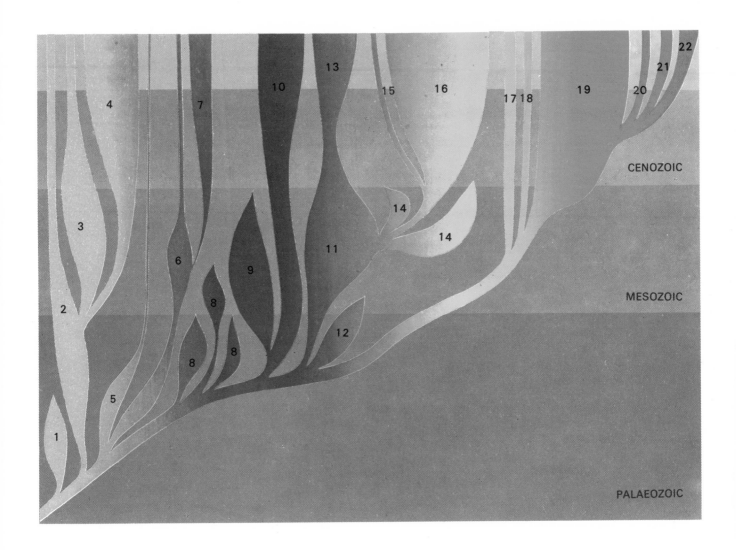

CENOZOIC

MESOZOIC

PALAEOZOIC

FISHES

1 Primeval fishes
2 Sharks and rays (Plagiostomi)
3 Ganoidei
4 Bony fishes (Teleostei)
5 Lungfishes (Dipnoi)

AMPHIBIANS AND REPTILES

6 Tailed amphibians (Urodela)
7 Frogs and toads (Anura)
8 Primitive amphibians
9 Dinosaurs
10 Turtles, tortoises and crocodiles (Hydrosauria)
11 Mesozoic reptiles
12 Primitive reptiles
13 Lizards and snakes (Lepidosauria)

BIRDS

14 Primitive birds
15 Running birds (Cursores)
16 Birds (Aves)

MAMMALS

17 Monotremes
18 Marsupials
19 Mammals
20 Prosimians
21 Apes (Simiae)
22 Man (Hominidae)

3   Down from the family tree

In this chapter we shall consider how much is known at present about fossil primates (that is to say, apes and man), beginning with fossil prosimians and the derivation of the anthropoids from them, and ending with the first representatives of the genus *Homo* ('man'). For the most part we will be concerned with the evidence from the Miocene and Pliocene periods, the times of greatest diversification of the apes and man.

Prosimians — ancestors of our ancestors

Prosimians are first known from the fossil record at the beginning of the Tertiary era, that is about 70 million years ago. They were small tree-living creatures with claws rather than nails, a projecting snout and poorly developed stereoscopic vision. They are distinguished mainly on the basis of their teeth and skulls, for in most other respects they resembled the insect-eating animals from which they originated.

In the Palaeocene several prosimian families are known. All of these had peculiar specializations of the teeth in one form or another — for example, rodent-like incisors or large serrated premolars. The best-known of the Palaeocene primates is *Plesiadapis,* known from both Europe and North America. It was a squirrel-like animal, with large rodent-like incisors,

Homo habilis, 'handy man'—a reconstruction from the finds made by L.S.B. Leakey in the Olduvai Gorge in Tanzania.

and claws instead of nails. The only really characteristic primate feature of *Plesiadapis* and other Palaeocene species is their flat, low-crowned cheek teeth with low, rounded cusps. These are so similar to the teeth of later, Eocene prosimians that despite the specializations just mentioned, they are almost certainly closely related.

By the Eocene several new kinds of prosimians appeared and radiated widely. The best-known of these are *Adapis* and *Notharctus,* the European and American forms respectively of the family Adapidae. They retained some primitive features not now found in living prosimians such as the tarsiers and the lemurs, but by this time they had also developed many of the specializations that characterize later primates, for instance reduced snouts, forward-pointing eyes protected from behind by a bar of bone and providing overlapping fields for stereoscopic vision, relatively larger brain size, nails instead of claws, and grasping hands and feet.

As well as the adapids, the ancestral tarsiers first appeared during the Eocene. Some of these developed odd specializations of the teeth and some were quite primitive, but the most interesting group of European tarsiers, of which *Necrolemur* is an example, remained relatively unspecialized. Another group, the Omomyidae, was widely spread in North America, and in many respects the members of this group are the most generalized of the Eocene prosimians and the ones most likely to have given rise to the ancestors of the higher primates.

The number of prosimian primates in the fossil record began to decline after the end of the Eocene. It is probable that as the lorises and lemurs developed their rather aberrant specializations of teeth and limb bones they became side-tracked from the main stream of primate evolution and were not able to compete with the evolving monkeys and apes.

Baboons, typical representatives of the Old World monkeys.

Early anthropoids

The earliest anthropoid primates known from the
fossil record are from the Oligocene period, in Egypt.
They were first discovered at the beginning of this
century in the Fayum region in deposits that were
laid down between 40 and 30 million years ago. There
are at least two groups of higher primates represented
in the Fayum. One group, the Parapithecidae, left no
descendants, but the other main group includes
Aegyptopithecus ('Egyptian ape') and *Propliopithecus*
('early greater ape'), which were almost certainly
ancestral to all the living Old World monkeys, apes
and man. *Aegyptopithecus* is from slightly later

deposits and is more advanced than *Propliopithecus,*
from which it was probably descended. Both look like
miniature apes, but while *Propliopithecus* is still quite
generalized and could have given rise to any or all of
the monkeys, gibbons, or great apes, *Aegyptopithecus*
had apparently already started on the evolutionary
route leading to the apes (chimpanzees, gorillas, and
orang-utans) and man.

Aegyptopithecus has typically ape-like teeth, with
large projecting canine teeth, upper molars with four
cusps and lower molars with five, and the cusps are
low and rounded. The lower jaw is deep and heavily
built as in apes and unlike prosimians. The skull has
some primitive features, such as the elongated snout,
but the eyes are completely closed in behind by bone.
This is related to the increased importance of the eyes
in higher primates, and is unlike the condition found
in prosimians. The ear region, however, is primitive.
The limb bones are quite specialized, showing that
Aegyptopithecus may have been a climber most similar
to the South American howler monkeys of today.

Fossil apes

The first known apes, which were probably descended
from *Aegyptopithecus,* were the dryopithecines ('forest
apes', a subfamily of the Pongidae). *Aegyptopithecus*
itself is sometimes included in the dryopithecines,
but the spread of this group was in the Miocene
period, 22 — 5 million years ago, rather than in the
Oligocene. The first dryopithecine ever discovered
was *Dryopithecus fontani* from middle Miocene
deposits in France. From the same period, but only
very rarely from the same deposits, came another
group of European Miocene apes called *Pliopithecus*
('greater ape'). These have long been thought to be
fossil gibbons, but they were already too specialized
and they evidently represent a side branch of the
gibbon family rather than a direct ancestor. One other
European ape was *Oreopithecus* ('mountain ape'),
which is a complete enigma. It had elongated hands
and arms, as do living apes, but it had such specialized
teeth that clearly it too was not ancestral to any living
species.

The earliest evidence so far available is from the
early Miocene of East Africa. For the greater part of
this century fossil dryopithecines have been coming
from Miocene deposits in Kenya, and more lately

Aegyptopithecus, *which lived around 30 million years ago, was the probable precursor of the living apes (chimpanzees, gorillas and orang-utans).*

Dryopithecus *('forest ape'), representative of the most widespread group of primitive apes 25 — 10 million years ago. This reconstruction is based on a fossil found in France.*

Uganda also, mainly as a result of the efforts of L. S. B. Leakey. Six dryopithecine species are now recognized for the Miocene of East Africa, and these are divided into three groups: *Proconsul, Rangwapithecus* and *Limnopithecus.* In addition there is a single species assigned to the gibbon family and called *Dendropithecus* ('tree ape').

All the early Miocene apes had basically similar teeth to those of the living apes. The teeth have the so-called dryopithecine pattern of grooves separating the cusps, and the cheek teeth all have characteristic shelf-like thickenings of the molar teeth, the presence of which distinguishes them from later dryopithecines but which is sometimes found in living apes.

We have no evidence at the moment which would enable us to link any one of these Miocene apes with any of the living great apes. One suggestion that has been made is that *Proconsul africanus* is directly ancestral to the chimpanzee, and *Proconsul major* is the forerunner of the gorilla. *Dryopithecus fontani* was also considered as a possible ancestor of the chimpanzee, but we now realize that the Miocene apes have so much variation that although one of them was almost certainly ancestral to some or all of the living great apes, it is not possible to say which species this was.

The teeth of the early Miocene *Dendropithecus* are similar to those of modern gibbons and its limb bones have begun to become elongated as in living gibbons, but it probably did not swing from branch to branch as they do. However, its anatomy indicates that the specialized gibbon anatomy could have

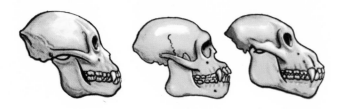

Comparison of the skulls of (left to right)
Aegyptopithecus, Pliopithecus *(another European ape)*
and Proconsul — *all of the Miocene epoch, 22 — 5 million*
years ago.

Oreopithecus bambolii *('mountain ape'), long-armed,*
tree-living, is probably an evolutionary dead end, not
ancestral to any ape. Its fossilized remains, from which
this reconstruction was made, were found in an Italian
coal mine.

evolved from it later, and the evidence suggests,
therefore, that *Dendropithecus* was directly ancestral to
the gibbons.

As far as we can tell, the ecology of the early apes
was very like that of monkeys. Although their teeth
and some features of their skulls are ape-like, their
limbs resemble those of the monkeys and their
movements in the trees must have been like that of
living monkeys. This idea is supported by the fact that
the environment in which the Miocene apes lived
resembled present-day monkey habitats in many
respects. The great areas of highlands were not
present in Africa in the early Miocene, but there were
a number of large volcanoes rising above the forest
lowlands. The dryopithecines probably lived both on
the slopes of these volcanoes and in the lowlands as
well. The environmental changes associated with the
formation of these volcanoes may have provided the
impetus for the spread and diversification of the
dryopithecines at this time.

The apes of today

There are four species of great ape living today. They
are the chimpanzees *(Pan troglodytes, Pan paniscus)*,
which occur in Central and West Africa, the gorilla
(Gorilla gorilla), which inhabits the Central African
forests, and the orang-utan *(Pongo pygmaeus)*, the
largest form of Asian anthropoid ape, which lives in
the forests of Borneo and Sumatra. The gibbons and
siamangs form a separate family, Hylobatidae, which
is included among the anthropoid apes in the wider

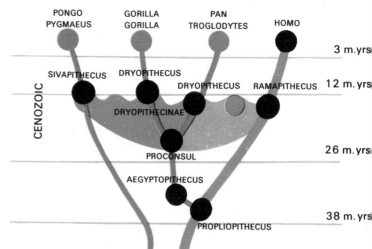

Molar teeth of ape (top) *and man. They can be distinguished by the number of points, or cusps: in man and his precursors there are five, separated by a Y-shaped fissure.*

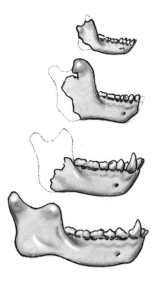

Comparison of the size and shape of the jaws of Propliopithecus, Pliopithecus, Parapithecus *and* Dendropithecus. *Such comparisons of teeth and jaws are valuable aids in identifying fossil remains.*

Dendropithecus ('tree ape'), ancestor of the gibbons, is shown swinging from branch to branch as the gibbons do, though its arm bones show that it was not fully adapted to this way of moving about the forests.

meaning of the term. There are six extant species of gibbons, so that they are more numerous than all the other anthropoid apes put together. They are usually placed in two genera, *Hylobates* with five species and *Symphalangus* with one.

The gibbons are in some respects an intermediate group between the monkeys and the great apes and man. They are more primitive in the form of their teeth and the structure of their skulls than the great apes, so they provide a good model for comparison with fossil apes, but in the rest of the body they are highly specialized. They have very long fore and hind limbs which enable them to move habitually with just

two limbs, either swinging by the forelimbs or walking on the hindlimbs. They also have an arboreal and social mode of life in the mountain forests of India and Malaysia that is unique among primates. The small family groups of one male and one female with their offspring are strongly territorial and stay together for long periods of time in one patch of forest.

The rarest anthropoid species today is the orang-utan. Orang-utans live in small family groups

ground, but the chimpanzees, and even more so the gorillas, live mainly on the ground, where they move by what is called 'knuckle-walking', that is they support their weight on the knuckles of their hands rather than on the palms. This probably came about because the ancestors of chimpanzees and gorillas lived in the trees, perhaps similar in adaptations to the orang-utan today, and their present form of life was forced on them by their increase in size and perhaps because of the competition with the diversifying monkeys.

The diminishing numbers of wild gorillas still alive inhabit the deep forests of Central Africa and a few mountainous areas on the Congo—Uganda border. They are huge animals, about 2 metres high, and usually weigh well over 100 kg. Like their forebears, they are entirely vegetarian. Before the beginning of the Pleistocene, groups of gorillas probably roamed over a much larger area of Africa and may even have extended into tropical Asia, like their predecessors at the end of the Tertiary, but when the tropical forests receded from these regions, the gorillas also disappeared. Only where the vegetation and the climatic conditions remained the same have these specialized anthropoids persisted down to the present day.

Proconsul nyanzae, *a possible forerunner of the anthropoid apes, lived about 19 million years ago. It was named in memory of 'Consul', a chimpanzee at the London Zoo.*

One of the living great apes, and possibly man's closest relative: the chimpanzee (Pan troglodytes).

with only a few members and some of the males actually live solitarily. Their apparently anti-social mode of life may be partly due to the disturbance caused by the exploitation of the forests to which they are now restricted, and it is possible that in former times they lived in family groups similar to those of gibbons. There is, however, some evidence that the solitary nomadic life of the males at least is a well-established behavioural pattern even though its significance is not fully understood.

Because of their size all the great apes are to a certain extent ground-living. The orang-utan is the least so, only the large males coming frequently to the

A primitive form of social grouping: chimpanzees gathering food on the edge of an African forest.

Chimpanzees live in large communities in the tropical regions of Central and West Africa, from the grasslands of Senegal to the Congo forests. They are more numerous than gorillas because the social character of community life, and a varied diet (chimpanzees live on the most diverse fruits, roots and small animals) have enabled them to spread over a comparatively wide area. The chimpanzees have an open-group social structure which is based on a loose association of individuals or sub-groups. The whole association occupies a large home range, and the animals can either come together or spread out, as food or other factors dictate. The more wide-ranging individuals can discover new food resources to which they may call the other members of the association, particularly the females with young that by necessity are less mobile. This type of open social structure is extremely flexible. It allows the group to adapt to a wide range of environments, and it has been suggested that the social structure of the early hominids might have been similar. There is no direct evidence for this, but chimpanzees are man's closest living relatives and it is a conspicuously successful adaptation for large ground-living primates at the edges of forests, the habitat in which man is thought to have evolved.

The orang-utan (Pongo pygmaeus) *lives in family groups. Nearing extinction, they are now found almost entirely in Borneo, but one million years ago they also lived in mainland China and Indochina.*

First steps towards man

In the middle Miocene a group of apes became distinguished from the fossil apes by the development of a number of man-like characters. These man-like apes are put at present into three genera, *Sivapithecus, Gigantopithecus* and *Ramapithecus* ('Siva's ape, giant ape and Rama's ape'). The characters they have in common are mainly concerned with their jaws and teeth and the way these are used in feeding and

chewing, so that we can also draw inferences on their diet. They have rather large cheek teeth with massively built jaws and small canines and incisors, which implies that their diet was coarser and more abrasive than that of the early apes. The environments occupied by these forms was also different, open woodland and savannah rather than forest, and this is consistent with their coarser diet.

This group of advanced apes was very widespread during the middle to late Miocene. It is known from

Czechoslovakia to China, but it is best known from India, Pakistan and Turkey, where it was represented by at least seven species. One and possibly two species are also known from Africa, but for the most part it seems to have been a European and Asian group, rather than African, although undoubtedly it had its origin from one of the earlier African species.

The earliest and most primitive member of this group of advanced apes is *Sivapithecus.* The earliest occurring species of *Sivapithecus* from Turkey is very similar to *Proconsul* from the early Miocene, and the latest species, known from Greece and Pakistan as well as Turkey, approaches *Gigantopithecus* in size. *Gigantopithecus* was the biggest anthropoid ever known, and its height, estimated from the size of its lower jaws, must have been at least 2 metres, slightly larger than the gorilla. The late Miocene species *Gigantopithecus bilaspurensis* was roughly

The gorilla (Gorilla gorilla), *the largest of the great apes, lives in the tropical forests of West and Central Africa.*

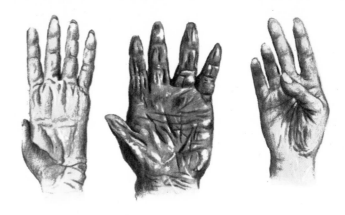

Comparison of the hands of (left to right) *the chimpanzee, the gorilla and man.*

contemporary with *Sivapithecus,* with which it may have competed for food and space, but the other known species, *Gigantopithecus blacki,* is known only from Pleistocene deposits of China, where it was contemporary with *Homo erectus.* There was probably no direct competition between *Gigantopithecus* and *Homo erectus,* for the former was a large, cumbersome vegetarian while *Homo erectus* was a fairly accomplished hunter, but their association raises the possibility that one of the animals hunted by *Homo erectus* was in fact *Gigantopithecus,* an ideal prey for a Stone Age hunter.

The *Sivapithecus-Gigantopithecus* lineage, with its latest representative a contemporary of *Homo erectus,* is not likely to have given rise to man. The third genus of this group, however, was less specialized in many respects than the other two genera, and based on this rather negative evidence *Ramapithecus* becomes the best candidate for a human ancestor. Several species of *Ramapithecus* may be present in the middle to late Miocene deposits of Kenya, Turkey, Hungary, Russia, India, Pakistan and China, but all are alike in having large, flat-crowned, steep-sided molar teeth and rather small canines and incisors, features that are close to the condition in man.

The resemblance between *Ramapithecus* and the apes is so strong that it seems reasonable to ask how it can be called a human ancestor. As man evolved from the apes, his first ancestors could be expected to be almost exactly like the apes that were living at that time, the dryopithecines. The difficulty is to pinpoint the adaptations which started them along the evolutionary route which has led to modern man. It is

thought that the most important first adaptations were connected with feeding on a diet of small objects such as seeds, and these adaptations would have included modifications of the jaws and teeth for crushing and grinding. Of all the Miocene apes, *Ramapithecus* is alone in showing these features, which is why it can be considered the most likely ancestor of man.

From ape to ape-man

From the time of the latest known species of *Ramapithecus* (14 — 10 million years ago) to the time of the first australopithecines (3 — 2 million years ago) there lies a gap in the fossil record of at least five million years. Exactly what happened during that time is not known, for we jump from the hominid-like but still mainly ape form that is *Ramapithecus* to the fully fledged hominid *Australopithecus africanus.*

There are two types of australopithecine, which are best recognized by separating them into two genera, *Australopithecus* ('southern ape') and *Paranthropus* ('almost man'). *Australopithecus* was first described as long ago as 1925 by Raymond Dart, who had brought to him a skull of a young child that had been found during mining operations at Taung cave in South

Reconstruction of the head of Gigantopithecus, *seen in profile. Fossils have been found in India and China.*

◁ *Peking man and* Gigantopithecus *could well have encountered one another. This largest ever of the primates reached a height of well over six feet and must have weighed nearly four hundred pounds. Despite its fearsome appearance, however, it was an inoffensive vegetarian.*

Gigantopithecus *was an evolutionary dead end, and became extinct about half a million years ago.*

Africa. Dart identified the skull as being a very primitive form of hominid, but it quickly became the centre of a storm of controversy because, hitherto, the few hominid fossils known had all been essentially modern in appearance and a fossil with so many apparently ape-like characters was not considered likely to be a human ancestor. Time, however, has proved Dart more right than wrong; *Australopithecus africanus,* which is now known in much greater detail from two other South African caves, Sterkfontein and Makapansgat, is seen unequivocally to be a hominid, although the fact that it lived alongside more advanced hominids would seem to exclude it from being directly ancestral to modern man.

The other type of australopithecine, found also at first in South Africa, is the more robust form named *Paranthropus robustus.* It is frequently put in the same genus as *Australopithecus,* but we prefer here to recognize two genera because of the major differences between the two species, particularly in their feeding adaptations. *P. robustus* was first found in 1938 in a cave in the Transvaal called Kromdraai.

Ramapithecus, the most likely candidate for the ancestor of man, lived about 14—10 million years ago. The massive jaws and small, human-like teeth suggest that its diet was varied and included tough vegetable matter.

Australopithecus *('southern* ▷ *ape') comes at least five million years later than* Ramapithecus *in the fossil record. Already we can see the development from ape to man beginning. In breaking up animal bones to get at the marrow they must have been very early tool-users.*

Exceptionally for South Africa, this cave was not discovered as a result of mining but it is exposed on the face of a gently sloping hillside. The roof of the cave has been removed over the years by natural erosion, and almost the entire contents of the cave are awaiting excavation. This is far from being the case at the nearby Swartkrans cave, the other main source of *P. robustus* fossils, where most of the contents of the cave have been removed and destroyed during mining operations. The first of a long series of fossil discoveries at Swartkrans was made in 1948 by Robert Broom, who also described the Kromdraai remains, so that *P. robustus* is as well known as *A. africanus*. Also like *A. africanus*, *P. robustus* is contemporary with more advanced hominids.

Later work in East Africa has greatly increased the number of australopithecines known. The first major discovery, in 1959, was a skull from Olduvai Gorge which L. S. B. Leakey named *Zinjanthropus boisei* ('Zinj man', *Zinj* being the Arabic name for East Africa). In fact it represents a robust australopithecine similar to *P. robustus,* so that it is more generally classified now as *Paranthropus boisei*. No specimens of *A. africanus* have been found at Olduvai, but it is known in northern Kenya, together with *P. boisei,* from deposits of a similar age to the east of Lake Turkana (formerly Lake Rudolf) and in southern Ethiopia from the Omo River deposits.

Reconstruction of an adult Australopithecus africanus. *From fossil skulls, as well as the bones of legs and feet, it can be deduced that they walked upright.*

Overleaf: *A group of australopithecines in the open steppe lands of southern Africa.*

First find of Australopithecus. *Discovered at Taung, in Botswana, in 1924, it can have been no more than nine years old when it died; it is often called 'the Taung baby'.*

The time span covered by these fossil localities in South and East Africa is approximately 3 to 1 million years ago. Generally speaking the robust australopithecines seem to occur in slightly later deposits than the gracile, more slender *A. africanus* but for most of their existence the two forms overlapped, although there is no evidence that they ever actually lived at the same time in the same place. It is possible that they did so, and one form may even have preyed on the other, but there is no direct evidence that this occurred.

The gracile australopithecine, *A. africanus,* was a relatively lightly built animal. It was probably no more than 1.2 metres (4 feet) tall and had a small brain of about 400 — 500 cc (compared with averages of just under 400 cc for chimpanzees and 1300 cc for modern man). The structure of its limb bones shows that it probably walked upright on two legs, in contrast to the four-footed walk of most other primates. Its Miocene ancestors discussed earlier in this chapter, the dryopithecines and probably also

Paranthropus boisei, *one of the most massive and robust of the australopithecines.*

Paranthropus *species seem to have been almost entirely vegetarian, living on green plant parts, edible roots and birds' eggs.*

Ramapithecus, are at present thought to have been four-footed, so it has advanced greatly from the dryopithecine stage. This is perhaps the strongest evidence that the australopithecines belong in the family of man, and this is supported also by the structure of the skull: the foramen magnum, the hole through which the spinal cord passes, is known from a number of skulls to have faced directly downwards, not coming out of the back of the skull as in four-footed animals, and the reduction in size of the neck muscles also shows that the skull was balanced on top of the spinal column. These changes suggest an upright posture and definitely indicate an upright, two-legged walk. The teeth of *A. africanus* were basically human and differed from the primitive condition in apes, particularly, for instance, in the structural changes of the premolars and canines.

The robust australopithecines, *P. robustus* and *P. boisei,* differed from the gracile ones in having larger and more heavily built skulls. Their brain size was between 500 and 600 cc, rather bigger than that

Paranthropus robustus — *reconstruction from a skull found in South Africa.*

of the gorilla, and the surface of the skull was expanded by ridges and crests for the attachment of the large head muscles. The most conspicuous of these was the sagittal crest, a bony ridge running along the top of the head like the one often present in gorillas. This crest increased the area of attachment of the main chewing muscles, which must therefore have been greatly enlarged and were associated with correspondingly enlarged jaws, the lower jaw particularly being a massive and heavily buttressed bone. The teeth also were greatly enlarged, particularly the cheek teeth, the premolars and molars, but the front teeth, the incisors and canines, were by contrast greatly reduced. Compared with *A. africanus,* the cheek teeth were larger in the robust australopithecines and the front teeth were smaller, so that their proportions were completely different, and this difference is important in interpreting the feeding habits of the two types. The rest of the skeleton of the robust australopithecines suggests that they also walked upright, and that they were substantially bigger than *A. africanus,* maybe as much as twice its body size.

The differences between the gracile and robust australopithecines are of the same kind as are often observed today between males and females of one species. This is true, for example, in modern man, in which the female is smaller and more gracile than the

male. If size were the only consideration, it could well be the case in the australopithecines that the gracile ones represent females and the robust ones males, but there are other differences as well. Gracile australopithecines are of course smaller than the robust ones in most dimensions, but their front teeth, their incisors and canines, are actually slightly larger. Their premolars are not merely different in size but they are very different in shape as well. Their skull is not just less robust, it is a different shape, and moreover there are a number of skulls, less robust than the typical robust individual but retaining the same shape, that could be robust females, and these are quite different from the gracile australopithecines. Finally there is little direct evidence that both types of australopithecines may have lived together at one time in one place. In South Africa gracile australopithecines occur at Sterkfontein and Makapansgat and robust australopithecines at Kromdraai and Swartkrans, and even though some of these sites are close together it would be odd for males only to be present at one place and females only at another. In East Africa both occur in the same deposits, but because many of these sites have not yet been systematically excavated it is not known whether they occur together at any one time-level.

We must assume, then, that the two types of australopithecine did exist as separate species. The question we must ask now is, how did they react to each other's presence? Even if they never actually met there must have been some interaction, because they both lived in similar habitats and had similar types of food available to them. It has been suggested that the robust form might have been a strict vegetarian whereas the gracile form might have been more of a scavenger, eating whatever it could but depending more on scavenged or hunted animal food than on vegetation. The evidence for this is based on the differences in the teeth mentioned earlier: the large cheek teeth of the robust australopithecines are well adapted for chewing up large quantities of tough

vegetable matter, while the more man-like teeth of the gracile australopithecines are more suitable for a mixed diet similar to man's today. If this were the case the two types of australopithecine may not have competed directly with each other, since their food requirements were completely different, and they may have lived side by side in mutual tolerance, much as the chimpanzee and gorilla do today in some parts of Africa.

Many of these problems about the relationships of the australopithecines to each other, and to more advanced hominids living at the same time, would be resolved if there were any evidence to show whether or not they used tools. It has been claimed that the australopithecines made fairly elaborate implements from animal bones and horns, but while this may very well be true the evidence in favour of it is weak. Where stone tools are found with australopithecine remains there is nearly always evidence of another, more advanced, hominid in the same deposits, and it cannot be certain whether it was this advanced hominid that made the tools or the australopithecine. Just because the other hominid is more 'advanced' it is usually assumed that it was the tool-maker, but there still remains the possibility that *A. africanus* at least could also make tools.

Homo habilis, 'handy man', was a meat-eater but not yet a successful hunter. Depending much on game killed by other predators, he would have had to beat off scavenging vultures; his powerful, grasping hands were well fitted for weapons.

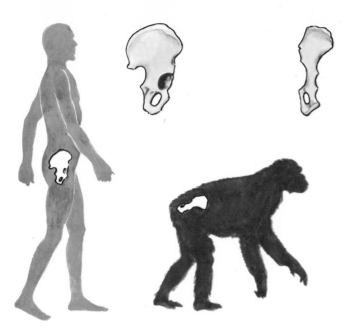

'Handy man' of East Africa

The advanced hominids present in the same deposits as the australopithecines form a third line of hominid evolution alongside those of the robust and gracile australopithecines. These advanced hominids are usually put in the genus *Homo*, that is the same genus as ourselves, but before going on to describe them we must look briefly at their origin. Did *Homo* evolve from an australopithecine or is there yet another branch of hominids from which perhaps both

One of the biggest differences between the skeletons of bipeds and of quadrupeds is in the shape of the pelvis: in man the weight-bearing blade is broad and the socket for the thigh-bone points downwards; in the chimpanzee, although it sometimes moves on two legs, the blade is relatively smaller and the socket points downwards and backwards.

Homo habilis *was likely to have been a tool-maker. Crudely shaped and chipped stones have been found with* habilis *fossils, but this may be due to chance.*

◁ Homo habilis *may have depended more on animal meat than did* Paranthropus. *But hunting skills would have taken many generations to develop; until the invention of arrow head and hand-axe (not found with* habilis *fossils), he would have killed only the slower and smaller creatures.*

47

australopithecines and *Homo* evolved independently? The answer seems to be 'yes' to the latter alternative, but the evidence for it is so new that it has not yet been completely written up. Two areas in East Africa are particularly important in this respect, because they have fossil-bearing deposits that are older than those at the sites so far discussed. They are Hadar, in the central Afar, Ethiopia, and Laetolil near Olduvai Gorge in Tanzania. Both are Pliocene in age and are dated at around 3 million years ago or even older.

The hominids from these sites do not appear to be australopithecines, for they mix very advanced features of the dentition with a number of primitive characters that are reminiscent of *Ramapithecus*. The cheek teeth are remarkably similar to later members of *Homo,* but the canines and front premolars are

A group of Homo habilis *gathering berries, eggs and roots, which, together with small animals, made up their staple diet.*

characters they actually appear more man-like than any of the Pleistocene australopithecines, so that they could equally well be ancestral to *Homo,* that is to modern man.

The first hint that there were *Homo*-like hominids living in the first part of the Pleistocene came in 1949 when the first *Telanthropus* ('distant man') mandible was described from Swartkrans. Several additional specimens have been found since, and it is now clear that *Telanthropus* is really the same thing as *Homo.* The best-known discoveries of very early *Homo* were made by L. S. B. Leakey at Olduvai Gorge, where, soon after the *Zinjanthropus* child's skull had been found (p. 39), some even more exciting discoveries were made of a partial skull and mandible that have been called *Homo habilis* ('handy man'). These were from a slightly lower level than *Zinjanthropus,* but further finds in the 1960's were made at both higher and lower levels, so that altogether *Homo habilis* ranged in age from nearly two million years ago to just over one million years ago.

Homo habilis was more advanced than the australopithecines in a number of ways. It had a larger and more complex brain, probably greater than 600 cc but not exceeding 800 cc in presently known specimens. Its teeth were rather smaller, but with some differences in shape as well compared with the australopithecines. Its limb bones were much closer to those of modern man, showing that it was a fully upright biped, and habitually walked on its two legs without using its arms. One of the first specimens found at Olduvai Gorge was a nearly complete set of foot bones, and these are so like the foot of modern man that, together with the other limb bones found subsequently, they show that *Homo habilis* could walk and run in a way very like modern man. The individual bones are rather smaller and less robust than in modern man, however, so that in over-all size *Homo habilis* was comparable with or slightly smaller than the West African pygmies, that is about 1 to 1.2 metres in height.

The hand of *Homo habilis* is also known from early discoveries at Olduvai Gorge. The bones indicate that

ape-like in shape, although in size they are small, and comparable with *Australopithecus africanus.* The limb bones are similarly intermediate, most resembling *A. africanus* bones in size but with some primitive features, for instance of the hip bone. These primitive hominids make good ancestors for *Australopithecus* and it seems quite clear that they are closely related, but what is so surprising about them is that in many it had a powerful hand, well able to make the stone tools with which the specimens were associated. Some degree of association with stone tools occurs for all of the presently known *Homo habilis* discoveries, and it must be almost certain that it was the maker of the tools, although there is some doubt, as mentioned earlier, about whether the australopithecines may also have been tool-makers.

There is, then, good evidence that *Homo habilis* was a tool-maker with a large brain, powerful grasping hands, and a walk very like that of modern man. It is known from excavations to be associated with butchered remains of animals, so that it apparently put all its newly evolved adaptations to use in a hunting form of life. It may indeed have hunted, among other things, the australopithecines, but it is likely that at this early stage of adapting to a hunting existence *H. habilis* was not a very successful hunter and must have depended to a large extent on other kinds of food, particularly, for instance, scavenged meat stolen from other predators, small mammals,

insects, birds' eggs, and roots and berries and other vegetable matter.

Both australopithecines and *Homo habilis* appear to have lived in open country or wooded environments, not in forests or thick woodlands. In this they are quite different from their Miocene ancestors, and it was probably this shift away from forest life that began the trend towards the unique specializations of present-day man. Probably the early adaptations were mainly concerned with diet, for the type of food available in tropical savannahs is very different from forest foods: the vegetation is not as luxuriant, leaves and roots are coarser or less succulent, and there are fewer plant species. For this reason the early adaptations of the evolving hominid line increased the grinding capacity of the teeth, as was described earlier for *Ramapithecus,* and these adaptations were present in even more developed form in the australopithecines, particularly *Paranthropus.*

As a result of this change in diet, early man would have had to cover much wider areas in his search for

Above: Homo habilis *in
a family group. At that time,
three million to one million
years ago, this would have been
the basic social unit, as it still
is today with the orang-utan.*

food, so that changes in his locomotion would be sure
to follow. Exactly why the changes that did occur
resulted in walking on two feet, when most other
animals that have similarly changed just became more
efficient quadrupeds, is not known, but it very likely
had something to do with freeing the hands for
carrying or collecting food. Wider use of the hands
perhaps led to greater complexity of the brain for the
control of hand manipulation, and these together
provided the framework for the manufacture and use
of tools. This is the stage reached by *Homo habilis* and
now we go on to consider the stages beyond, up to
modern man.

*East African landscape and
animals at the beginning of
the Quaternary period, around
one million years ago.
Baboons, giraffes, antelope
and hippopotamus had by
then evolved into their present
forms.*

51

Distribution of anthropoids and hominids

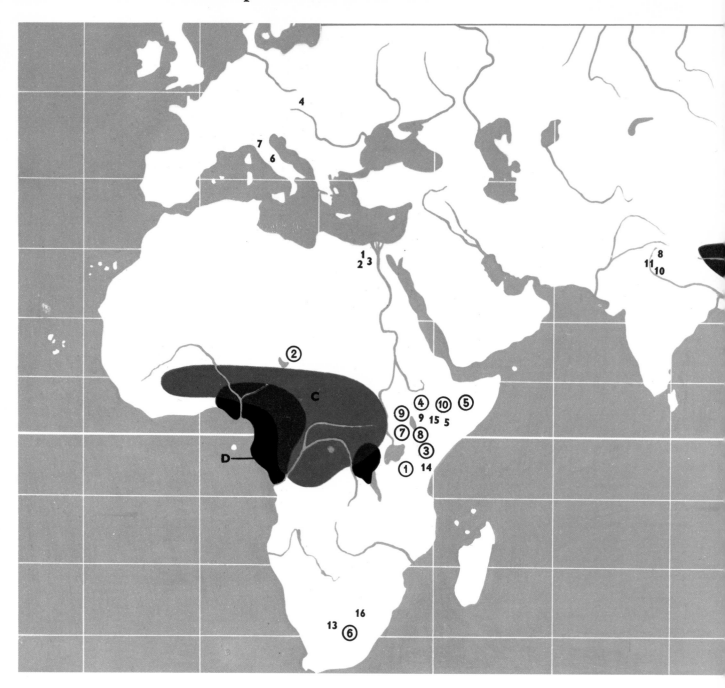

Anthropoids

A	Gibbon *(Hylobates)*	Illiger	1811	Malay Peninsula
B	Orang-utan *(Pongo pygmaeus)*	Lacépède	1779	Borneo
C	Chimpanzee *(Pan troglodytes)*	Oken	1816	Tropical Africa
D	Gorilla *(Gorilla gorilla)*	Geoffroy	1852	Central Africa

Extinct anthropoids and hominids

1	*Propliopithecus*	Schlosser	1911	Oligocene, Egypt
2	*Aegyptopithecus*	Simons	1965	Oligocene, Egypt
3	*Limnopithecus*	Hopwood	1933	Miocene, Egypt
4	*Dryopithecus*	Lartet	1856	Miocene, Old World

The Olduvai Gorge, Tanzania, where Homo habilis *was found.*

10	*Sivapithecus*	Pilgrim	1910	Miocene — Pliocene, E. Africa & India
11	*Sivapithecus giganteus*	Pilgrim	1915	Miocene, India
12	*Gigantopithecus*	von Koenigswald	1935	Pliocene, China
13	*Paranthropus robustus*	Broom	1938	Pleistocene, S. Africa
14	*Paranthropus boisei*	Leakey	1960	Pleistocene, E. Africa
15	*Paraustralopithecus aethiopicus*	Coppens	1949	Pleistocene, E. Africa
16	*Australopithecus africanus*	Dart	1925	Pliocene, S. Africa

Where Homo habilis **has been found**

①	*Homo habilis*	Olduvai, E. Africa	1962
②	*Tchadanthropus uxoris*	Lake Chad, Central Africa	1966
③	*Homo habilis*	Lake Rudolf, E. Africa	1972
④	*Homo habilis*	Omo, S. Ethiopia	1972 — 3
⑤	*Homo habilis*	Afar, E. Ethiopia	1974
⑥	*Homo capensis*	Swartkrans, S. Africa	1953 — 75
⑦	*Homo habilis*	Koobi Fora, Kenya	1972 — 6
⑧	*Homo ergaster* (or *H. erectus*)	Illeret, Kenya	1972 — 5
⑨	*Homo* sp.	Lothagam, Kenya	1975
⑩	*Homo* sp.	Hadar, central Ethiopia	1975 — 6

5	*Proconsul africanus*	Hopwood	1933	Miocene, E. Africa
6	*Oreopithecus bambolii*	Gervais	1872	Miocene — Pliocene, S. Europe
7	*Pliopithecus*	Gervais	1849	Miocene — Pliocene, Europe
8	*Ramapithecus punjabicus*	Pilgrim	1910	Pliocene, India
9	*Sivapithecus africanus*	Le Gros Clark and Leakey	1950	Miocene, E. Africa

4   Man takes the stage

The real home of man, in other words where the human race and human society originated and underwent their first stages of development, was not just a single region, but was probably the great open spaces of the continents of Europe, Africa and Asia. In these open spaces, wooded steppes and grasslands formed almost unbroken belts stretching across the three continents of the Old World at the end of the Tertiary and throughout much of the Quaternary period.

At the beginning of this century it was thought that only some parts of southern and eastern Asia were the cradle of mankind. Finds made in this region, particularly those from Java and Peking, pointed to the possibility of a Far Eastern origin for the evolution of the hominids. An alternative suggestion was that the cradle of human society lay in central Asia, between the Caspian Sea, the Pamir and the Altai mountains. But these and other hypotheses have been abandoned with the discovery of large numbers of bones and cultural relics of early hominids from Africa, some of which date from well over one million years ago. So the focus of attention in studies of hominid evolution has switched more recently to southern Africa and the Rift Valley areas of eastern Africa, especially to the countries of Ethiopia, Kenya and Tanzania. However, potassium-argon dates recently obtained from Java suggest that man may, after all, have existed in south-east Asia nearly two million years ago, a date comparable with those obtained from African sites.

It is unlikely that large human populations inhabited the continents of Europe, Asia and Africa before one million years ago, and even as recently as the Upper Pleistocene (about 100,000 years ago) human groups must still have been thinly scattered since social evolution progressed only hesitatingly. This was because although man's physical evolution progressed from the level of *Homo erectus* to *Homo sapiens,* even the most physically evolved men of the Pleistocene were still leading the way of life of nomadic hunters and gatherers.

So extremely slow evolution of man and his culture, and the gradual colonization of the wooded steppes of the Old World, are characteristic of the Lower and Middle Palaeolithic. It was only during the last 10,000 years, after the end of the Pleistocene and the Upper Palaeolithic, when the ice sheets had retreated from the northern parts of Europe and Asia, that new ways of life, in particular the domestication and exploitation of plants and animals, led to a great growth in human populations and a faster rate of technological and social change. And by this stage man had also established himself for the first time in the continents of America and Australasia. It is impossible today to determine exactly the details of movements of these prehistoric groups or of their way of life, but much information can be reconstructed by using evidence from modern populations and from the remains left by prehistoric societies.

At first the general trend was for mankind to spread in the direction of least resistance, where food was most abundant and where the climate and environment were most congenial. Later on, as he became more adaptable, man was able to venture into the less hospitable areas such as the tundra-lands, deserts and tropical forests.

Who is 'man'?

The problem of defining when 'man' first appeared is an extremely difficult one since it depends on which definition of 'man' we choose to adopt. The

Java man—Homo erectus erectus ('upright-standing man'). This reconstruction is based on the finds by Dubois and von Koenigswald in Java, at Sangiran and Trinil, two places on the Solo river about 40 miles apart.

classification of the African finds of the
australopithecines and *Homo habilis* is still under
intensive discussion since many new finds have been
made recently, but the species *Homo erectus,* known
from Africa and Asia and, probably, Europe, is

generally regarded as the first recognizable human.

Homo erectus probably evolved from hominids like
Homo habilis; both species are known from Africa,
while in Java and China four sub-species of *Homo
erectus* have been recognized. In the Lower

modjokertensis from Modjokerto in eastern Java, and the *Homo erectus lantianensis* fossils from Lantian, China. *Homo erectus modjokertensis* represents the oldest and most primitive form of *Homo erectus* known from Asia and perhaps, as some authorities believe, the whole world. Somewhat later in date (but nevertheless approaching a million years old) are the Lantian remains found between 1963 and 1974 in the Chinese province of Shensi. These hominids had brain volumes of 700—800 cc, greater than those of the australopithecines and the *Homo habilis* fossils from Olduvai, but less than the later forms of *Homo erectus.* The brain volume is, in fact, comparable with that of certain fossils from Koobi Fora (East Rudolf), Kenya, such as the skull known, from its find number, as '1470' (see p. 44). Population movement between the Asian mainland and south-east Asia would have been possible for most of the Pleistocene since there were then land-links between what today are islands, and so the Lower Pleistocene representatives of *Homo erectus* in China and Java were probably related parts of the same stock.

The original finds of *Homo erectus* were the famous finds from Trinil in Java, now classified as *Homo erectus erectus.* 'Java man' lived in the area over 500,000 years ago during a period of extensive volcanic activity and earthquakes. This species of early man was known for many years as *'Pithecanthropus erectus'* (the 'erect ape-man') and there are intriguing reasons for this choice of name. The name *'Pithecanthropus'* had been coined by the German biologist Ernst Haeckel before any actual remains of this type of early man had been found. Haeckel was one of the most important followers of Darwin and he came to the conclusion, along with other supporters of the evolutionary theory of the origins of man, that prehistoric man (already known in the form of the fossils of Neanderthal man) was not the earliest human being to have existed. According to Haeckel, between prehistoric man and the anthropoid apes there must have existed another form — still only hypothetical in Haeckel's time — to which he gave

Pleistocene, primitive forms of hominids, perhaps equivalent to *Homo habilis,* precede the typical *erectus* fossils of the Middle Pleistocene. These primitive forms include the *'Meganthropus'* fossils and other finds which have been assigned to *Homo erectus*

the name *'Pithecanthropus alalus'* ('ape-man without speech'). Acting on this hypothesis the Dutch physician Eugene Dubois decided to search for the remains of the oldest ancestor of man in southern or south-eastern Asia. After two years of fruitless searching on Sumatra, Dubois went to Java where, in 1890—91, he discovered the remains to which he gave the name *'Pithecanthropus erectus'* (*'erectus'* because the remains included thigh-bones which indicated that this form of early man walked upright).

Some scientists considered that *'Pithecanthropus'* was human, others that it was an ape, and yet others suggested it was a genuine intermediate form between ape and man. Differences of opinion between anthropologists and zoologists were particularly marked, with the former claiming that the bones belonged to an ape, and not a human being, whereas the latter argued the opposite case. When the bones were examined by a group of research workers, however, most of them were obliged to admit that the find was genuinely ancient and they agreed with Dubois's report of 1894 which claimed that the skull was much larger than that of any anthropoid ape, though it was smaller than the skull of modern man, having a brain volume with less than two-thirds that of a present-day human skull. The back part of the skull was less rugged than in apes, while the most complete thigh-bone had human dimensions and its owner could obviously have walked upright.

Many other remains of related forms have been found in Java during this century. Most have come from the valley of the river Solo and the ancient volcanic dome of Sangiran. These include remains of *Homo erectus erectus* (over 500,000 years old), *Homo erectus modjokertensis* (over 1 million years old) and the remains of the later Pleistocene Solo man from Ngandong (classified as a sub-species either of *Homo erectus* or of *Homo sapiens*).

The other famous remains of *Homo erectus* from Asia are those from Choukoutien, near Peking in China. In 1928 a Chinese geologist, Pei Wei-Chung, discovered the first skull of a fossil hominid which was originally named *'Sinanthropus pekinensis'* ('Chinese man of Peking'), a name which had already been given to a previously discovered fossil tooth. Many more finds of Peking man were made, representing dozens of men, women and children who had lived in or near the Choukoutien caves perhaps 400,000 years ago. Here on the slopes of small hills, with a view of the great Chinese plains stretching away to the sea, lived families of *Homo erectus pekinensis*. Because of the nature of their preservation in cave deposits we have much more information from the remains about the way of life of Peking man than is the case for Java man. So we can be much more certain about the hunting and other abilities of Peking man, and because the Peking remains date from rather later than the typical Javanese *Homo erectus* fossils we should also not be surprised to find that the Peking *Homo erectus* fossils are in some ways more advanced, having on the average a larger brain, and a smaller face and teeth.

△ *Three subspecies of* Homo erectus *can be compared in reconstructions based on fossil finds:* modjokertensis *from the Lower Pleistocene of Java, over a million years old;* erectus *from the Middle Pleistocene of Java, over half a million years old; and* pekinensis *(Peking man) from the Middle Pleistocene of China, 400,000 years old. In Peking man we begin to see signs of a larger brain, and a smaller face and teeth.*

Flake tools like these were found with the remains of Peking man in the Choukoutien cave, China.

Wooden spears with fire-hardened tips were used by Homo erectus *as effective hunting weapons.*

The first human communities

In physical appearance the *Homo erectus* peoples of Asia were not too different from modern man, being perhaps 160—170 cm tall to judge by the size of their thigh-bones. They probably lived in small groups which were dominated by a few males. They lived by gathering and hunting and were no doubt led by the strongest and fittest male, who acquired and maintained his position not merely through physical strength but through his ability as a hunter and leader. The average age at death of these early men may have been less than thirty years, with women probably outliving men since they would have been less exposed to the danger of mortal injury. This was because there was probably a truly human division of labour operating by this stage, with the men primarily responsible for hunting and defending the group, and the women responsible for collecting edible plants, berries and small animals, as well as rearing the children.

The family and community life of primitive man must have evolved exceedingly slowly. At the

australopithecine stage communication would probably have been at a level comparable with that of modern apes, consisting of sounds, gestures and facial expressions. The australopithecine social structure may also have been comparable to that found in apes or monkeys. We cannot be sure when the basic human social unit consisting of a man, a woman and their children developed, but many experts consider that it may have evolved, along with true human language, at the stage of *Homo erectus.*

The spread of man to more temperate areas must have been a very slow process and as long as the level of cultural sophistication remained low it must have been a precarious existence. At this stage groups of primitive humans, isolated and widely scattered, would have found it difficult to achieve much in the way of communication from one group to another, whether for an exchange of ideas or for exchanges of individuals for social reasons. On the other hand, the diverse geographical and climatic conditions in the various parts of the Old World to which these groups spread helped them to adapt and thus, on a long-term basis, to evolve. For instance, if a group of primitive people moved to a place where the plants and animals

were unfamiliar, they had to learn to adapt themselves quickly to their new surroundings; if they did not, they inevitably died out.

There is no good evidence for the existence of man in Europe before about one million years ago, although the recently excavated site of Sandalja in Yugoslavia may be of that age. But the most positive evidence of an evolved form of *Homo erectus* or an early form of *Homo sapiens* comes from the sites of Heidelberg, Vértésszöllös and Petralona. The remains attributed to *Homo erectus heidelbergensis* from Germany and *Homo erectus palaeohungaricus* from Hungary are rather fragmentary whereas the Petralona skull from Greece is much more complete although less certainly dated.

'Heidelberg man', also known as *'Maueranthropus'* or *'Protanthropus heidelbergensis',* is represented by a massive lower jaw found in 1907 in a quarry at the village of Mauer, near Heidelberg. The jaw dates from the Middle Pleistocene, perhaps 500,000 years ago, but no artefacts were found in direct association with the fossil. The Hungarian find from Vértésszöllös which consists of the back part of a skull and some teeth, comes from a slightly later period, perhaps

◁ *As man slowly learned to communicate, on a level higher than ape-like grunts, such fundamental skills as the shaping of stone tools would have been passed on from generation to generation.*

Heidelberg man—a European form of Homo erectus. *This reconstruction is based on finds from the Middle Pleistocene of Germany, perhaps half a million years old.*

Bands of Homo erectus *must have always lived close to a water supply—both for their own needs and because water attracted game.*

A group of Homo erectus *gathering food and hunting in the jungle around the volcanoes of Sangiran, in Java.*

400,000 years ago, but together with this find there were some rather primitive artefacts and remains of hearths. There is some disagreement among experts as to whether the Petralona skull, which is perhaps of the same age, is *Homo erectus* or *Homo sapiens*. It is in some respects rather advanced for an *erectus* skull although the face, upper jaw and base are very massive.

Older remains of European Lower Palaeolithic tools are known from near the town of Slatina in Romania; Přezletice (which also produced a human tooth fragment) and Stránská Skála in Czechoslovakia; Westbury-sub-Mendip in England; and Vallonet in France.

Finds attributed to *Homo erectus* have recently been made at Bilzingsleben in East Germany, where parts of the front and back of a skull were found together with many artefacts, and from the French site of Vergranne.

The way of life of Homo erectus leakeyi *in the Rift Valley areas of East Africa was very like that of the closely related Java man.*

At Ngandong, in Java, a number of skull-caps of Solo man (a probable subspecies of Homo erectus *) have been found. So many are there that some sort of head-hunter's display has been suggested. Perhaps early man resorted to cannibalism for ritual purposes or when food was scarce.*

Colonizing Africa and the Far East

Turning back to Africa, it is remarkable to note that virtually the whole of this vast continent was colonized by man as early as the Lower Pleistocene. As we have seen, forms perhaps ancestral to *Homo erectus* are known from the oldest levels at Olduvai Gorge in Tanzania *(Homo habilis)*, from Koobi Fora, Kenya (for example the '1470' skull), and from Swartkrans in South Africa. The latter finds, described as *'Telanthropus capensis'*, came from a site already famous for finds of the robust australopithecine *Paranthropus*, but the lower jaw and skull parts of *'Telanthropus'* are clearly more like those of *Homo* and may represent a link between the gracile australopithecines and *Homo erectus* — comparable in fact to *Homo habilis* and '1470'. But true examples of *Homo erectus* are also known from Olduvai, e.g. the skull-cap now assigned to *Homo erectus leakeyi* which may be one million years old, and the newly-described skulls of *Homo erectus* from Koobi Fora, which are probably even older.

Homo erectus mauritanicus — originally named *Atlanthropus* ('Atlas man') — was discovered in Middle Pleistocene deposits at Ternifine in Algeria. As well as three jawbones and a parietal bone (sidepiece of the skull), there were also large numbers of stone tools, including nearly 150 hand-axes. This discovery of an ancient workshop furnished important evidence on the method of manufacture of the hand-axes which were such common elements in the tool kits of man during the Lower Palaeolithic. In 1954—5 fragments of a lower jaw of a similar form of early man were found at the Sidi Abderrahman cave near Casablanca in Morocco. Another find from the same area was the jawbone from the Thomas quarry

*The North African form of early man—*Homo erectus mauritanicus, *here seen in the foothills of the Atlas* Mountains—*made stone tools. But these were still a long way from the controlled, expertly shaped tools of later times.*

which was found in 1969. This is later in date than the Ternifine finds but tools found with it, and the form of the Thomas jawbone, suggest links with the Algerian fossils. Yet another recent find of late Middle Pleistocene age from Morocco is a skull found at Salé in 1971, which shows an interesting mixture of advanced and primitive characteristics.

Finds of Middle Pleistocene age have been very rare in south-west Asia, but between 1959 and 1963 some fragmentary material was discovered at 'Ubeidiya on the western bank of the river Jordan. These remains, which can probably be assigned to *Homo erectus,* include teeth and skull fragments. It is interesting to note that they come from an area which represents the northern extension of the African rift-valley system, which suggests some sort of connection with similar fossils found in eastern and southern Africa.

In the Far East, the hand-axes which are so common at African Middle Pleistocene sites have not been found with *Homo erectus* fossils. The Choukoutien people, using quartz chopping tools, made objects which look at first sight considerably cruder than similar things from Africa of equivalent date (perhaps 400,000 years ago). However, the inhabitants of the Choukoutien caves did not have access to the excellent flint, chert and lava materials available to their contemporaries elsewhere in the Old World, and this may account for their apparent lack of sophistication. Similar tools and implements have been found in Java, Burma and the Punjab, dated to some time in the Upper Pleistocene, so these peoples must have wandered far, and persisted for a long time.

The fact that tools have not been found in earlier levels in China *(Homo erectus lantianensis)* and in Java *(Homo erectus modjokertensis* and *'Meganthropus')* should not be taken to mean that these earlier forms of man had no tools. Such things may not have been recognized, or the sites may not have contained cultural remains, some of which may well have been made of perishable materials such as wood. Stone tools were already very much a part of man's adaptation in Africa two million years ago, and this suggests that *Homo erectus* probably used tools from the earliest stages of his evolution in Asia. Additionally there are similarities of form in fossils of *Homo erectus* from Africa and Asia which suggest that they were closely related and stemmed from

Outside the Choukoutien cave, near Peking. By this stage in man's development there was probably some sensible division of labour, with the women responsible for rearing the children and for collecting plants and berries for food.

a common stock. There is no evidence at the moment that Europe was populated by early forms of *Homo erectus,* and it is uncertain whether the continent was colonized from Asia or from Africa. Some anthropologists even maintain that the earliest European fossils, from sites such as Heidelberg and Vertésszöllös, were distinct from *Homo erectus* populations in the rest of the Old World, and evolved independently into the more advanced species *Homo sapiens.*

The early hunters

But all the populations of the Middle Pleistocene seem to be characterized by an efficient adaptation to hunting and processing game. Tools such as hand-axes were suitable for many different purposes and could be used for stabbing, cutting, scraping and digging, but man increasingly began to develop more specialized implements which required greater skill in production and use. This was probably paralleled by a more complex social system, involving a greater division of labour between men and women. *Homo erectus* was perhaps organized in large family troops,

which later gave way to even larger units such as tribes. The social system must have been more developed and complex than that of *Homo habilis* and *Australopithecus,* and the greater degree of co-operation between troop members would have been a great advantage in hunting large animals and defending the group. This meant that *Homo erectus* was able to hunt animals as large as elephants or rhinoceroses, and it is even possible that *Homo erectus* in China encountered the large ape *Gigantopithecus* (see p. 36). This creature, once considered as a possible ancestor for man, is now thought to have been a large but probably peaceful herbivore.

Although *Homo erectus* was apparently an efficient hunter, there must nevertheless have been times when large animals were scarce, and in those times small animals would have been trapped or these early men may have resorted to scavenging. But in times of drought even plants may have become scarce, and then the larger social units of *Homo erectus* would perhaps have disbanded to exploit the remaining scattered food resources. Some anthropologists have suggested that these peoples may have resorted to cannibalism in times of food shortage, at least to the extent of eating the flesh of already dead troop members.

There is disputed evidence of cannibalism in the case of the Choukoutien finds of *Homo erectus pekinensis.* As already mentioned, remains of at least forty individuals of various ages were excavated from the cave. All of the skulls had incomplete bases when discovered, and many arm and leg bones were broken lengthwise. Some even showed signs of being burnt. It was suggested that the skulls had been broken open to extract the brains and that other bones had been split to extract the marrow. However it should be remembered that the base of the skull, along with the face, is the part which is most readily damaged by the gnawing of animals or by earth pressure after burial. Such damage can be seen in less ancient skulls, where there is no suggestion of cannibalism. In the case of the split arm and leg bones it is possible that they were crushed, or chewed by carnivores such as hyenas. Nevertheless it is still difficult to account for the fact that the bones were burnt, but regrettably all the Peking fossil material was lost during the Second World War and therefore it is not available for study by modern techniques. Compensation for this tragic loss is partly made by more recent finds of material at the Choukoutien site by Chinese scientists, but detailed reports of these finds are not yet available.

As has been mentioned already, several of the sites of *Homo erectus* finds show evidence of the use of fire. There is evidence from Africa that fire was being used over a million years ago, but it is not certain that man was able to create fire at that stage. Fire would have been an important ally of man as he moved into more temperate areas, and the evidence from sites such as Vertésszöllös and Choukoutien suggests that by 400,000 years ago man had harnessed fire for warmth and protection and was probably also using it for hunting in order to drive animals into areas where they could be more easily slaughtered. There is excellent evidence of the latter practice from Middle Pleistocene sites in Spain dating to about 300,000 years ago.

Thus by the production of stone tools and then by the mastery of the power of fire, early man was progressively separating himself from nature. Instead of being another animal subject to the laws of nature, man was developing an independence from, and even dominance over, parts of his environment.

Heads of Peking man (full face) and his mate.

The discovery of how to make use of natural fires, and keep them burning, was an important advance in man's adaptation to his environment, about half a million years ago.

Where *Homo erectus* has been found

This is where Homo erectus *fossils were first found, in 1891, at Trinil by the river Solo.*

Key

1	*Homo erectus modjokertensis*	Java	1938—39
2	*Homo erectus erectus*	Java	1891—1977
3	*Homo erectus heidelbergensis*	Mauer, W. Germany	1908
4	*Homo erectus pekinensis*	Choukoutien, China	1927—66
5	*Homo erectus lantianensis*	Lantien, China	1952—64
6	*Homo erectus leakeyi*	Olduvai, Tanzania	1961
7	*Homo erectus*	Koobi Fora, Kenya	1975
8	*Homo erectus mauritanicus*	Ternifine, Algeria	1954—73
9	*Homo erectus palaeohungaricus*	Vertésszöllös, Hungary	1965
10	*Homo erectus*	R. Jordan, Israel	1959—69

5   Enter Homo sapiens

The earliest members of our own species, *Homo sapiens,* appeared in the Old World during the later Middle Pleistocene, perhaps 300,000 to 400,000 years ago. There was no sudden change from the late *Homo erectus* populations, but instead a gradual evolution towards a more advanced form of man. For this reason there is in fact considerable difficulty in placing some of the fossils at this stage into one or other of the two species. Fossils of 'archaic *Homo sapiens*' (by which is meant the past members of our own species which were more 'primitive' than modern man) ranged in date from perhaps 300,000 years ago up to about 40,000 years ago. The main changes from the species *Homo erectus* to *Homo sapiens* involved a further reduction in the size of the face, jaws and teeth accompanied by an increase in the size of the braincase.

But there was also an increase in the complexity of human behaviour, to judge by the new kinds of tools being produced. There is greater evidence of the use of tools made specially for tasks such as butchering meat, scraping skins and working wood. Wooden spears with fire-hardened tips seem to have come into general use and traps and pitfalls were probably constructed to capture game. There is also good evidence that man was already able to build huts of wood or large bones with a covering of branches or animal skins. Skins may also have been used as clothing in the less hospitable areas of the world. The greater sophistication in the way of life of archaic *Homo sapiens* perhaps also indicates an increase in ability to communicate through language, and in the complexity of social structure. In the later stages of

Neanderthal man, an early representative of our own species, Homo sapiens. *The braincase was large, and the nose was human instead of ape-like.*

the evolution of *Homo sapiens,* but still before the appearance of modern man, there is definite evidence of religious beliefs, ritual behaviour and even the beginnings of artistic expression.

Fossil Europeans

Two of the earliest undisputed examples of our own species are the skulls from Steinheim in Germany and Swanscombe in England. The former skull, discovered in a gravel pit near Stuttgart in 1933, has a small and rounded braincase, but there are large brow ridges above the relatively robust face. No definite tools have been found at the Steinheim site, but in the case of the Swanscombe site, near the River Thames in Kent, large numbers of tools, including well-made hand-axes, had been found there long before human fossils were discovered in 1935, 1936 and 1955. These three fossil bones fitted together to form the back part of a skull, similar in form to that of Steinheim but a little larger and with thicker walls. Because of similarities in the animal remains found with them these specimens are known to date from an interglacial, probably the 'Holsteinian' (the 'Hoxnian' in England, see p. 224), which may have lasted from 250,000 to 200,000 years ago. A lower jaw discovered at Montmaurin in France in 1949, and the Bilzingsleben remains recently found in East Germany, may also date from the same stage.

The Bilzingsleben, Montmaurin and Vertésszöllös remains (mentioned in the last chapter) were all found together with stone tools, but without any hand-axes, and similar industries (such as the 'Clactonian' in England) existed before the main hand-axe industries such as those from Swanscombe. But the Clactonian could not have been the ancestor

of the later hand-axe industries since an even earlier hand-axe stage existed *before* the Clactonian. So the possibility arises that there were distinct cultural groups or tribes of early *Homo sapiens* persisting for vast periods of time, some making various forms of tools but no hand-axes, others producing so-called 'Acheulean' industries with many hand-axes. Such differences could even be due to tribes adapting to different ways of life, for instance in forests as distinct from grasslands. But the fossil remains themselves do not reveal any marked differences which could support the idea of distinct tribes evolving completely separately over many thousands of years.

The degree of physical variation of the Middle Pleistocene is nowhere more apparent than at the site of Arago in the French Pyrenees. The site has produced many tools (but no good hand-axes) and various fragmentary human fossils, all apparently

dating from an early stage of the glaciation (the 'Saalian' or 'Riss') that followed the warmer stage in which the Swanscombe and Steinheim peoples lived. The most important of these 200,000-year-old fossils are two jawbones and the well-preserved bones of a face. One of the jawbones and the face are very massive, even suggesting that these remains could represent *Homo erectus*. But the other jawbone and some of the teeth found there suggest that the Arago people were in fact early examples of *Homo sapiens* who link the earlier Holsteinian fossils with the later Neanderthal fossils. The variation present in the Arago fossils is almost certainly due to the fact that for once both rugged males and less rugged females are represented at a site.

Later fossils which continue this evolving line of early *Homo sapiens* are known from Germany, France, Czechoslovakia and Italy. At Ehringsdorf near

Weimar in Germany, parts of skulls and teeth were found between 1908 and 1925, and in 1926 an unusual find of a natural cast of a human brain was made at Gánovce in Czechoslovakia. The site of Saccopastore in Italy produced two skulls between 1929 and 1935 accompanied by remains of rhinoceros, straight-tusked elephant and hippopotamus. And several sites in France such as Lazaret, Abri Suard (La Chaise) and Fontéchevade have provided similar material which can be considered as ancestral to the later Neanderthal peoples. These various remains date from the period 150,000 — 70,000 years ago and though the individual

◁ *Several times during the last million years, thick sheets of ice reached as far south as the Thames and the Volga, in America almost to the latitude of Kansas City and St Louis.*

A Neanderthal hunter. Clubs, hand-axes and sharpened spears show how man's developing brain tackled the problems of killing for food.

The tundra environment around the edges of the ice sheets provided grazing for large herds of reindeer and mammoth.

*These large herds of animals sometimes provided rich hauls
for the Neanderthal hunters.*

fossils tend to be fragmentary, when considered together they provide evidence of an evolutionary development through reduction of the braincase, together with an expansion of the size of the brain.

Outside Europe similar developments were probably occurring, but the evidence is far less complete. This is partly because archaeologists have worked most intensively in Europe, but their work has been made easier by the fact that many of these early Europeans used caves for shelter, and these were excellent places for tools and bones to both accumulate and be preserved. Hence we can say with some confidence that fire was being used in Europe for warmth, for protection and for cooking 150,000 years ago, and that the human populations were able to construct huts of wood and skins to give additional shelter from the less pleasant aspects of the European climate.

One of the earliest finds of Homo sapiens *—Steinheim man, who lived some 200,000 years ago in what is now Germany.*

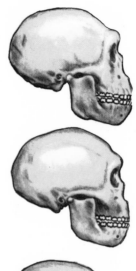

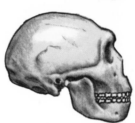

An early African, Homo sapiens rhodesiensis: *this reconstruction is based on the skull found at Broken Hill in Zambia.*

A comparison of three reconstructed skulls of fossil Homo sapiens. *Reading down they are: the Steinheim skull (200,000 years old), an early Neanderthal (100,000 years old) and a late Neanderthal (50,000 years old).*

Hardening spear points over ▷ a fire.

The other side of the world

In the Far East, it is believed, the *Homo erectus* populations of China and Java were continuing to evolve in parallel with their cousins in Europe and Africa. The skull found by Woo Ju Kang in the Lion Hill cave near Mapa, Kwantung, in 1958 dates from over 100,000 years ago and seems to be at the same evolutionary stage as the European peoples of the same date. It shows features reminiscent of its presumed ancestor *Homo erectus pekinensis,* but nevertheless has a more evolved braincase resembling the later Neanderthals.

In Java, remains of perhaps a dozen individuals were found at Ngandong on the Solo river. Though resembling the earlier *Homo erectus erectus* and *Homo erectus modjokertensis* fossils, the eleven skulls seem somewhat more evolved. For a long time after their discovery in 1931—3 they were considered to be

Upper Pleistocene in date (probably less than 100,000 years old), but more recent and similar discoveries from Middle Pleistocene deposits in Java suggest that these fossils could be well over 200,000 years old. They have been classified as either *Homo erectus soloensis* or *Homo sapiens soloensis* by various authorities, but in terms of the evolutionary level of the fossils the former name seems to suit them better.

Apart from controversy over their classification they are also of interest for the possible evidence they provide for cannibalism in the Pleistocene. Many of the skulls are said to show injuries, some inflicted long before death, and some at the time of death. Additionally it is remarkable that only skull parts and two shinbones were found at the Ngandong site, whereas teeth and jawbones usually survive well as fossils. This suggests that early men may have been responsible for the unusual selection of material discovered. Speculation about damage to the base of the skulls has led once again to the idea that this area was broken open to extract the brains for cannibalistic practices. However, a note of caution needs to be added, as in the case of the Peking fossils: there are alternative explanations for this kind of damage.

Early man in Africa

In Africa, an area which has produced so much evidence of the earlier stages of man's evolution, there is strangely little evidence of fossil man during the last half-million years. The descendants of *'Homo erectus mauritanicus'* of North Africa may be

represented by Moroccan material from Salé and Sidi Abderrahman, as mentioned in the last chapter, and by jaw fragments from Rabat, perhaps dating to 200,000 years ago. But for more complete material from the late Middle Pleistocene and the early Upper Pleistocene we have to turn once again to Ethiopia and areas south of the Sahara. The region of the Omo river valley in southern Ethiopia is famous for its australopithecine fossils, but in an expedition led by Richard Leakey three later hominid fossils were also recovered, from the Kibish beds. The most complete specimens are a fairly complete skull lacking its face, and a less complete skull which nevertheless has fragments of the face, jaws and the rest of the

A group of Neanderthalers outside the Kůlna cave in Czechoslovakia, some 50,000 years ago.

A Neanderthaler family group moving camp to more favourable hunting grounds. As hunter-gatherers they naturally had to lead a nomadic existence.

skeleton. The former specimen is remarkable for its unusual combination of archaic and advanced features. The back of the skull is like *Homo erectus* fossils, but the form of the frontal bone and the height and volume of the braincase make it quite clear that this fossil must be *Homo sapiens*. The other main find is remarkable for the modernity of the bones of the skull, jaw and skeleton. Apart from their robustness and large size they seem to qualify the specimen as a genuine early member of our own sub-species *Homo sapiens sapiens*. In fact if the suggested date of over 100,000 years is correct, this fossil represents *the* earliest example so far known of modern man.

Further south in Africa, a skull has recently been found at Ndutu in Tanzania. Although originally described as a form of *Homo erectus,* the fossil perhaps represents an equivalent of hominids such as those from Steinheim, Swanscombe and Salé. An African specimen which shows even clearer links with *Homo erectus* is the skull from Kabwe (Broken Hill) in Zambia. This specimen has been known for many years as 'Rhodesian man' since Zambia was formerly known as Northern Rhodesia — hence the fossil is classified as *Homo sapiens rhodesiensis*. It was found by a miner during mining operations in 1921 and was quickly recognized as one of the best preserved and most important fossil human relics. Unfortunately the excavation of the skull and a large number of other human and animal bones, as well as tools, could not be supervised by archaeologists, so the dating of the skull is rather uncertain. However, if it really belongs with the tools found there, which represent the 'middle stone age' African industry, it would now be regarded as dating from well over 100,000 years ago. Such a date fits its more primitive characteristics since it resembles Middle Pleistocene fossils from Europe (Petralona, Arago) and from Java (the Solo skulls). It could even be related to the skull assigned to *Homo erectus leakeyi* (Olduvai hominid 9 or 'Chellean man') even though they may be separated by up to a million years of human evolution. However the massive form of the brow ridges, face, palate and occipital ridge are balanced by the more advanced nature of the base and sides of the skull, and the volume of the braincase. Furthermore, none of the bones of the rest of the skeletons found at the site appear to be distinct from those of modern man,

Neanderthalers feeding in the Krapina cave, Yugoslavia. It has been suggested that some of the finds from this cave provide evidence for cannibalism.

Homo sapiens neanderthalensis —a portrait based on the famous find from La Chapelle, France.

although none certainly belong with the Rhodesian skull. Another related fossil is the less complete skull-cap and jaw fragment from Saldanha (Hopefield) in South Africa, which may date from 100,000 years ago. This find demonstrates the wide distribution of this type of early *Homo sapiens,* which may be further represented at the site of Makapansgat in South Africa and Eyasi in Kenya.

Neanderthal man

Returning once again to the relatively rich fossil record of Europe, we arrive at the stage of the last glaciation, when for the first time substantial numbers of early humans were able to adapt to the rigours of life in a tundra environment. These peoples were the Neanderthals, and their main means of adaptation was their tool industry called the 'Mousterian'. (This type of industry was named after the site of Le Moustier in France.) But we now know that there was

◁ *Bones of large animals found at various sites suggest that Neanderthal hunters understood intelligent co-operation in hunting. The driven game, killed and butchered, would then be shared out among them.*

Even co-operative hunting must often have been a dangerous and bloody business.

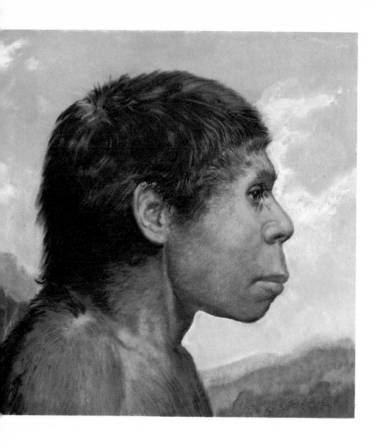

Portrait of a Neanderthaler boy, based on the burial shown opposite.

At Teshik-Tash in Soviet Central Asia, a burial was found in 1938, of which this is a reconstruction. A boy of about nine years of age had been carefully buried, and ibex skulls had been arranged around his grave. This seems to argue a surprising degree of sentiment and ritual, 50,000 years ago.

not one uniform type of Mousterian in the period from 70,000 to 35,000 years ago. Instead there were a number of well-defined separate industries which apparently maintained their distinctiveness through time and space. One was the so-called 'typical' Mousterian which contained certain recognizable 'type artefacts', occurring in fairly consistent proportions. Then there were the 'Quina-Ferrassie' industries which contained high percentages of thick scraper tools, and these were the industries found with the most typical fossils of Neanderthal man from France. There was also a 'denticulate' Mousterian with many saw-edged and notched tools of small size. Yet another distinct industry was the 'Mousterian of Acheulean tradition' with hand-axes which may represent a link back to those found in the previous interglacial stage, and even further back to the classic hand-axes found at St Acheul in France and Hoxne and Swanscombe in England.

It is a matter of great argument among archaeologists whether these variants merely represent special Neanderthal tool-kits for certain activities, for example wood-working, butchering meat, skinning carcasses, or whether there were

indeed different tribes of Mousterians who co-existed but maintained their distinctive cultures over periods of many thousands of years. Perhaps these groups were adapted to life in different environments, for the 'Mousterian of Acheulean tradition' seems to have been the only kind of Mousterian found in the rather distinctive British environments of the last ice age. Unfortunately we do not have good fossil remains of the manufacturers of each of these various types of Mousterian, and therefore we cannot easily assess how physically distinct they were.

The first physical remains recognized as 'Neanderthal man' were found in the Neander valley, Germany, in 1856. Because of the publication of Darwin's *Origin of Species* in 1859, the fossils were rapidly drawn into the debate on the evolution of man and various interpretations were made about their unusual nature. On the one hand they were regarded as a genuinely ancient record of a kind of man distinct from modern man, and at the other extreme they were considered to represent some kind of pathological freak. If the importance of the Gibraltar skull found in 1848 had been recognized much earlier, it would have been realized that there

Homo erectus soloensis — *reconstructed from a skull found at Ngandong on the Solo river, Java. Some experts believe that this is a Far Eastern Neanderthaler, but its date can be shown to be too early. Compare the head below, with its higher braincase and smaller face.*

European Neanderthaler, based on a find in France.

were similarities between the fossils from Neanderthal and Gibraltar, but it was not until many more finds had been described from sites such as Spy, Engis and La Naulette in Belgium, Šipka in Czechoslovakia, Bañolas in Spain, Malarnaud in France, and Krapina in Yugoslavia that talk of pathological freaks was finally silenced. And far more complete finds of skeletons from the sites of La Chapelle, La Ferrassie and Le Moustier in France (1908—20) led to the first full descriptions of the anatomy of Neanderthal man. Originally classified as *Homo neanderthalensis,* it is now generally agreed that the Neanderthal finds show much in common with other fossils of *Homo sapiens* from the Middle and Upper Pleistocene, and that therefore the most reasonable classification for them is as *Homo sapiens neanderthalensis.*

At first many of the early studies of Neanderthal fossils concentrated on the unusual nature of the Neanderthal skeleton and gave rise to a picture of Neanderthals as rather ape-like with a stooped, bent-kneed posture, toes which could grasp like those of apes, and an inferior brain, despite its large size. However, this one-sided picture could have been balanced by evidence from several French sites which demonstrated the concern of the Neanderthals for their dead, since they carefully buried them and sometimes placed materials such as meat or beautifully made flints within the grave. This suggests a belief in an after-life and a degree of spirituality for these cave-dwellers of 50,000 years ago. Furthermore, the graves were sometimes covered by carved stones or were within complex patterns of pits and mounds of unknown meaning. More recently, pollen has been found in one of the Neanderthal burials at Shanidar in Iraq, suggesting that brightly-coloured flowers were thrown on to the corpse at burial.

Evidence of other ritual activities comes from the sites of Drachenloch in Switzerland and Kudaro, Georgia (Soviet Union) where skulls of cave bears and deer had been collected and arranged by

Conflict between a Neanderthal hunter and a woolly rhinoceros — one of the animals that was well adapted to the harsh conditions of the ice ages.

A woolly rhinoceros caught in a pit-trap—another hunting device known to the Neanderthalers.

Neanderthals. In 1938 at Teshik-Tash in Soviet Central Asia a burial of a boy of about nine years of age was found, together with an arrangement of ibex skulls. In Italy a Neanderthal skull was found in the cave of Monte Circeo where it had lain undisturbed for over 40,000 years, lying base upwards in a ring of stones. This has led once again to speculation about cannibalism. The site of Krapina produced remains of many Neanderthals, consisting of broken and sometimes burnt bone fragments. However, recent studies suggest that the material does not all come from one level and may span 50,000 years of time, so the likelihood of there having been a great battle between different tribes, or a cannibalistic orgy, has been considerably reduced.

The Neanderthal 'race' seems to have had a widespread distribution in time and space. European fossils from Ehringsdorf and Saccopastore (perhaps over 100,000 years old) are probably some of the earliest examples of the group and the fossils from Amud and Tabun in Israel may well represent some of the latest examples (40,000 years old). These fossils share a distinctive group of characters. The skull of Neanderthal man was typically long but low in height, with a large braincase which was spherical in shape when viewed from behind. The average Neanderthal brain was larger than the modern average size but its proportions were somewhat different, and we have no

◁ *Neanderthal man hunted the cave bear — by guile and ambush, probably.*

The cave bear, cornered and rearing upright, would have been a good three feet higher than its pursuers, and must have been the most dangerous of the Neanderthal hunters' prey.

evidence of its internal development. The face of the Neanderthals was dominated by a prominent nose, and above the nose was a strong brow-ridge which was nevertheless smaller than in *Homo erectus* fossils. Some Neanderthal lower jaws show the presence of a bony chin. The rest of the skeleton was also distinctive, but not in any way ape-like. The European Neanderthals were especially short and stocky with thick-boned arms and legs, and they may have had similar proportions to modern Eskimos, though they were much more muscular. Neanderthal women were apparently much smaller than the men, but both sexes had an unusual type of hip-bone structure.

The Neanderthals of south-western Asia, e.g. those from Iraq and Israel, were less extreme in their characteristics and this has led to the suggestion that the more unusual Neanderthal features were expressions of an adaptation to the cold ice-age environment of Europe and Asia. The fact that the near-eastern and middle eastern Neanderthals were less 'extreme' has also led some anthropologists to suggest that they were in fact undergoing evolution into early modern men (represented by the skeletons from the sites of Skhul and Qafzeh in Israel), or alternatively that they were hybrids between the extreme Neanderthals and more modern populations. The situation is very complicated since most of these south-west Asian fossils (including the 'modern' ones) are associated with similar Mousterian cultures. The site of Qafzeh in Israel has yielded remains of over a dozen different individuals, from infants to adults, and several of them seem to have been buried with some accompanying ritual. These burials are thought to be more ancient than some of the Neanderthals (e.g. those from Tabun and Amud) which are perhaps 40,000 years old. If this dating is correct, it confirms

Burial of a Neanderthal hunter in the cave of Le Moustier—one of the earliest burials known to us.

Eight thousand feet up in the Alps, in a cave at Drachenloch, cave bear skulls were found, arranged in stone 'shrines'—evidence of some kind of ritual activity among the Neanderthalers.

the evidence from Omo that modern or near-modern forms of man had evolved from a pre-Neanderthal rather than a Neanderthal ancestor, and in fact co-existed with the Neanderthals, who could be regarded as 'brothers' to modern man rather than 'fathers'.

From elsewhere there is further evidence that modern man may not have evolved from the Neanderthals, and may already have existed when the Neanderthals lived in Europe. In Morocco there are three specimens from the site of Djebel Ighoud which may be 50,000 years old. Although primitive in some respects they seem somewhat closer to modern man than are the extreme Neanderthals. Further south there is evidence from the sites of Border Cave, Klasies Cave and Florisbad in South Africa that modern or near-modern forms existed there over 50,000 years ago. The Florisbad skull is the most robust of these specimens and has even been linked with the more ancient and primitive Kabwe (Broken Hill) skull. From Asia there is evidence of modern man from the Niah Cave, Borneo, dating from 40,000 years ago, and it now seems possible that by this date modern forms of man had already arrived in the New

Above: *Primitive man and the wonders of nature: we can only speculate on what Neanderthal man thought about the rainbow.*

◁ *Primitive man and the forces of nature: a tree struck by lightning could have been a danger or — before he learned how to make fire — a boon.*

World and in Australia. So instead of the Cro-Magnons — the Upper Palaeolithic people of Europe — representing the earliest examples of modern man, they were in fact only one part of a world-wide appearance of *Homo sapiens sapiens* which occurred before 30,000 years ago.

Where Neanderthal man and related forms have been found

Key

Pre-Neanderthalers and early Neanderthalers (400,000 — 70,000 years ago)

1 Swanscombe (England)	**9** Galilee (Israel)	**17** Teshik-Tash (USSR)	**24** Sidi Abderrahman and
2 Steinheim (W. Germany)	**10** Tabun (Israel)	**18** Kiik-Koba (USSR)	Djebel Ighoud (Morocco)
3 Montmaurin (France)	**11** Skhul (Israel)	**19** Staroselye (USSR)	**25** Diredawa (Ethiopia)
4 Fontéchevade (France)	**12** Amud (Israel)	**20** Subalyuk (Hungary)	**26** Ngandong (Indonesia)
5 Arago (France)	**13** Krapina (Yugoslavia)	**21** Šala (Czechoslovakia)	**27** Broken Hill (Zambia)
6 Ehringsdorf (E. Germany)	**14** Petralona (Greece)	**22** Kůlna, Ochoz and	**28** Saldanha Bay (S. Africa)
7 Gánovce (Czechoslovakia)	**15** Shanidar (Iraq)	Šipka (Czechoslovakia)	**29** Makapansgat (S. Africa)
8 Saccopastore (Italy)	**16** Behistun (Iran)	**23** Haua Fteah (Libya)	

26

The Neander valley (Neandertal), near Dusseldorf, where the fossilized remains of Neanderthal man were found.

Classical Neanderthalers (70,000—35,000 years ago)
Homo sapiens neanderthalensis (King, 1864)

30 Neandertal (W. Germany)	**36** La Ferrassie (France)
31 Gibraltar	**37** La Naulette (Belgium)
32 Bañolas (Spain)	**38** Spy (Belgium)
33 La Chapelle (France)	**39** Jersey (Channel Is.)
34 Le Moustier (France)	**40** Monte Circeo (Italy)
35 La Quina (France)	

6

The world of the Cro-Magnons

The history of *Homo sapiens* in the last 40,000 years has been one of accelerating change as each new discovery and invention built on the framework of existing knowledge. However, it was only in the last 12,000 years of man's evolution that the domestication of plants and animals gave the real possibility of a settled life with an assured food supply. Then followed the development of pottery, metalworking, the wheel, writing, and many other innovations of crucial importance to human progress. But before these significant developments all human peoples existed through hunting and gathering their food, essentially as their ancestors had done for two million years or more. Man spread across the whole habitable Earth, yet the story of this spread is only poorly recorded from archaeological remains.

We know from the discoveries of *Homo sapiens* fossils in Australia (Lake Mungo), south-east Asia (Niah, in Borneo) and North America (sites in Canada and California) that man's physical evolution had achieved a fully modern level by 30,000 years ago. But how much cultural evolution was there still to achieve? We can guess that human language was fully developed at this stage, but what of the power to abstract and symbolize, what of religious beliefs and social systems? Regrettably the evidence from most of the world is virtually non-existent. The Australian aborigines must have possessed boats in order to arrive in Australia at all. They were cremating their dead and producing cave art from a very early date but culturally they were not yet at an 'Upper Palaeolithic' stage as advanced as the Cro-Magnons of Europe — the next stage after Neanderthal man and the first recognizable representative of modern man,

Homo sapiens sapiens. However, the Cro-Magnons did not possess boats, let alone seagoing vessels capable of voyages of fifty miles or more. So we should beware of thinking that Europe and the Cro-Magnons were specially forward in the story of human progress.

After the ice-caps retreated in Europe there was a distinct decline for several thousand years from the cultural heights achieved by the late Cro-Magnons. What *is* important is that the areas of Europe and western Asia have preserved relics of the Cro-Magnons and their way of life so that they were available for proper excavation and study. Intensive excavations in other parts of the world may well produce records of prehistoric cultures every bit as impressive as the cave art of Lascaux and Altamira. So the Cro-Magnons should be regarded as representatives of the human progress which was probably occurring in parallel in many other parts of the world as well.

Modern man in ancient times

The Cro-Magnons were named after the first important finds from the Cro-Magnon rock shelter, in the Dordogne region of south-western France. These finds date from about 25,000 years ago and it was at this late stage of man's evolution that we have evidence of a great increase in man's ability to adapt to different environments and of many remarkable discoveries and inventions. At this stage, too, man was spreading for the first time to the continents of the New World (via north-eastern Asia) and to Australasia

Portrait of a hunter—Homo sapiens sapiens. This reconstruction of the first recognizable representative of modern man is based on the finds from the Cro-Magnon cave in France.

Overleaf: A Cro-Magnon encampment. There is no firm evidence for the use of the bow and arrow as early as this, but their invention has not been dated with any certainty.

(via south-east Asia). During the period which covers the Cro-Magnon settlement of Europe we have the first clear evidence of important developments such as the invention of the spear-thrower, the needle, sewn skin clothing, the harpoon, fishing equipment, the oil-lamp, personal jewellery, painting, engraving, sculpture and musical instruments.

The first Cro-Magnon finds were discovered in 1868, and they inevitably became involved in the debate about the antiquity of man. They were also the first significant finds from the Dordogne region of France which has since become such a centre of world prehistory. Here rivers have cut steep valleys through the limestone rock, and in the cliffs so formed erosion has produced many rock shelters (overhangs) and caves which were ideal homes for prehistoric animals and man, and which have continued to be used as shelters even in the recent past. In the Cro-Magnon rock shelter (named after an ancient hermit called Magnon) several men, women and children were buried some 25,000 years ago, including an old man who became, in a sense, the type of the whole Cro-Magnon 'race'. These fossil remains, like those found twelve years earlier in the Neander valley in Germany, assumed great importance in the debate about the antiquity of man. On the one hand they seemed to provide evidence of the coexistence of man and extinct 'antediluvian' animals (i.e. dating from before the Biblical flood) yet in contrast with the Neanderthal finds they provided evidence that truly modern man existed in ancient times.

Above: *Trapping and killing a mammoth must have needed the co-operation of a fairly numerous band of hunters.*

◁ *Towards the end of the last ice age, large herds of mammoth roamed the southern edges of the great ice sheets.*

In time many similar discoveries were made in the Dordogne region and from areas as far apart as the British Isles and Siberia. However, it was eventually realized that the Cro-Magnons dated from thousands of years *later* than the Neanderthal peoples, who had lived before them in the same areas and even in the same caves. And, unlike the Neanderthals, they shared the great majority of their physical characteristics with modern *Homo sapiens*. Their brain capacity was as large as, or in some cases even larger than, that of modern man (an average of about 1,450 cc) but the brain proportions were modern, rather than Neanderthal. The braincase was short, high and rounded, without the large brow ridges found in earlier fossils. The face was robust but essentially like that of modern Europeans (as was the skin colour, to judge by the slender evidence of cave paintings), and the lower jaw ended in a definite chin.

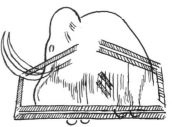

This cave painting from Bernifal, France, seems to show a mammoth caught in a pit. Was it hunter's magic, or can it be interpreted as instruction in mammoth-trapping?

Even after it fell into the pit, the mammoth probably took a long time to die. And then the hunters had to hack off the meat and carry it back to their camp.

Old Stone Age hunters on the track of a mammoth herd.

The term 'Cro-Magnon' is often used to refer to the populations who made the kinds of tool found in the Upper Palaeolithic, but it does in fact cover a wide variety of peoples who lived in Europe and western Asia for a period of over 20,000 years. So it should not be expected that they would have a uniform physical appearance or way of life, especially when one considers the differences which have developed in Europe in even a few thousand years of recent history. Nevertheless at one extreme some anthropologists have suggested that all the Cro-Magnons were of a basically similar physical type, while others have recognized many different races, even to the extent of identifying 'Eskimoid', 'Australoid' and 'Negroid' populations. But certainly even at the earliest stages,

30,000 years ago, there was a wide variation present in the Cro-Magnon peoples, as revealed by finds from the Dordogne region alone. The Cro-Magnon skeletons seem to represent slender, long-limbed individuals with broad, short and flat faces. In contrast, the slightly earlier find from nearby Combe-Capelle has a short, stocky build with a longer, narrower skull and a more projecting face. This diversity has even led some anthropologists to derive some of the Cro-Magnons from their predecessors in France, the Neanderthals. But such variation can be found in Cro-Magnon skeletons from all over Europe and western Asia, perhaps indicating the evolution of different 'races' in response to the very different environments of the last ice age.

Hunters and gatherers

The rich stock of large mammals which had been available to the Neanderthals was also available to their successors, the Cro-Magnons. But the Cro-Magnons were even better equipped to hunt the herds of reindeer, horse, mammoth, woolly rhinoceros and other large mammals which roamed the southern margins of the ice sheets. It was a strange world — an environment which we find difficult to visualize today since despite the low temperatures inflicted on Europe and Asia, a rich animal life was able to thrive. Present-day tundra areas such as Greenland and Lapland seem so barren, but it must be remembered that if the ice-sheets had moved much further south, their margins would have supported luxuriant vegetation because the more southerly latitudes would provide longer growing seasons and a more constant period of daylight throughout the year. This crucial difference meant

Hunting the bison. Lured or pursued into a marsh, this massive animal would have been at a disadvantage. Bison, often wounded or dead, figure largely in the cave art of western Europe.

In the tundra country of Scandinavia and northern Russia there is evidence that the hunter-gatherer's diet was eked out with birds. These could have been snared, or brought down with stones, or (though this is more doubtful) shot with bow and arrow.

that even when large herds were not available there were many more small mammals, birds and plants to be collected.

We can learn something of the probable way of life of the Cro-Magnon peoples of Europe by looking at modern peoples with a hunter-gatherer way of life, provided we remember that these present-day peoples have had a long period of social evolution in their own environments, and should not be regarded as 'remnants' of a Cro-Magnon stock which has remained in an unchanged 'Palaeolithic' state. Tropical hunter-gatherers could until recently be found in Asia (for example the Semangs of south-east

Asia and the Andamans of the Indian Ocean), in South America (e.g. many Amazonian Indian tribes) and Africa (the pygmies). However, 'progress' is inevitably eroding their natural habitats and rapidly changing their life-style. Perhaps more relevant to reconstructions of the Cro-Magnon way of life are the steppe and semi-desert type of hunter-gatherers such as the Australian and Tasmanian aborigines, the original inhabitants of Tierra del Fuego (at the southern tip of South America), and the Bushmen of southern Africa. All these peoples live (or in the case of the extinct Tasmanians, lived) in small bands which can exploit the scattered food resources of their environments; they use temporary dwellings as they have to remain mobile for much of their lives; they have little in the way of permanent possessions beyond the tools they need for hunting, gathering and

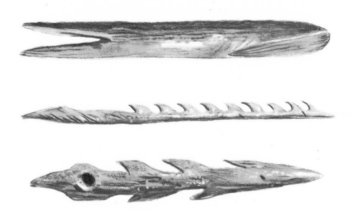

Bone harpoons and spearheads, made by Cro-Magnon hunters and fishermen. Even the invention of such a simple thing as the barb was a considerable advance.

Cro-Magnons in the northern tundra were protected, as they hunted the reindeer, by sewn skin clothing—another important development. These tunics, sewn from animal skins, are very like the parkas worn by Eskimos today.

preparing food; and they often hunt collectively when pursuing large game. But the simplicity of their material possessions (which is all that might survive for a future archaeologist to study) belies the complexity of their social systems and religious beliefs.

Parallels with the Cro-Magnons can also be provided by the hunter-fishermen of the temperate forest belts such as the Red Indian tribes of North America and various Eurasian peoples who existed into historic times. Meat was obtained by hunting forest game, and simple fishing techniques such as hooks, nets and traps were developed. The social system was based on family groups, and bigger groups such as totemic clans sometimes existed. Tents were used for summer dwellings, and winter shelters were

Within a supporting wall of mammoth tusks and bones, this Cro-Magnon hut was probably built of wooden stakes covered with animal skins. This drawing is based on remains found at a site in what is now Czechoslovakia. Conditions inside huts like this must have been cramped and smelly, but they were protection against harsh winter conditions.

Strange hybrid figures, part human, part animal, have suggested to some that a form of camouflage might have been part of the Cro-Magnon hunter's armoury. Arctic reindeer-hunters might perhaps have stalked their prey with antlers tied to their heads. (But for another guess, see p. 149.)

dugouts of a more permanent nature. Sledges were used for land transport, and birch bark and tree-trunks were used to construct boats. More specialized fishermen developed at the end of the Palaeolithic in the basins of great Siberian rivers such as the Ob (for example the Khants). Fish became the staple foodstuff for the whole year and hence fixed dwellings and settlements could evolve. Clothing was made from the skins of aquatic animals, and there was a much richer development of objects of material culture than would be found in the more nomadic hunter-gatherer groups.

Nearer the Siberian coast and in the Arctic areas of North America, a separate type of hunter-gatherer evolved, specializing in marine animals. The Siberian Chuckchee and the Eskimos of Alaska, Canada and Greenland are examples of this type. A good supply of game and fish allowed these people to remain in

The taiga—the marshy pine forest country of Siberia. Although herds of mammoth no longer roam there, the region is still rich in game, as it was 20,000 years ago.

one area for longer periods of time. Because of the lack of wood the Eskimos developed the igloo as a dwelling, and used animal fats for lighting and heating. Their clothes consisted of sewn skins and furs in several layers for extra warmth, and fur boots and snowshoes allowed mobility in a snow-covered environment. Dogs were specially bred for drawing sledges as land transport, and light skin boats (kayaks) were built for fishing and hunting. The way the Eskimos met the demands of their environment — especially their excellent hunting weapons — shows a resourceful adaptability equal to any of the peoples of the Upper Palaeolithic.

The reindeer hunter-breeder of the taiga and tundra country developed mainly in Asia. Peoples such as the Evenkoes and Lamuts used the reindeer as a draught animal, and it provided a valuable source of raw materials such as skin, sinew, bone and antler, besides meat. The Lapps have similarly developed a semi-pastoral existence, even using the reindeer to

As the ice sheets retreated, a rich and varied animal life flourished on their semi-arctic southern edges. Bears, as we know from cave art, were often the prey of Cro-Magnon hunters.

provide milk, but instead of a settled pastoral way of life they follow the migrating reindeer herds in a closer approach to the ways of their Palaeolithic ancestors. It is not thought that such an economy developed until after the end of the Palaeolithic, but many late Cro-Magnons in south-west Asia and North Africa were already approaching this way of life through reliance on one herd-species alone.

Tools and tool-makers

The main means of adaptation through which the Cro-Magnons were able to survive so successfully for 20,000 years as hunter-gatherers in Europe was by the making of flint tools, the various tool-making styles (or 'industries', as the archaeologists call them) being collectively known as the Upper Palaeolithic. As explained on page 225 the Palaeolithic (Old Stone Age) in Europe was divided into three supposedly consecutive stages called the Lower, Middle and Upper Palaeolithic stages. However, with a more complete record within Europe and the evidence of rather different cultures outside the area, it has become increasingly difficult to define the stages clearly.

The Upper Palaeolithic industries do share several features in common (for example the greater use of bone, ivory and antler as raw materials), but their main distinguishing characteristic is the preponderance of blade tools, produced by striking long, thin flakes of flint (or other raw material) from a core, probably by the use of a punch. These blades were then modified to produce specialized tools such

As success in the hunt was essential for survival, the training and initiation of young hunters must have been highly important in Cro-Magnon times. There is some evidence (see below) of initiation ceremonies, but the younger generation would also have been 'blooded' in the real thing.

A hunter of the Upper Palaeolithic, with his weapons. Flint or bone spearheads were bound to wooden hafts with vegetable fibres su.h as withies, or with skin thongs.

Deep in a cave at Montespan, France, a headless clay model of a bear was found, peppered with spear-holes. Perhaps it was the centre-piece of an initiation rite for young hunters, as, under the guidance of the medicine.man and lit by the leaping flames of a fire, they hurled their weapons symbolically at the skin-covered model to work up their courage for the hunt.

Above: *Not weapons alone aided Cro-Magnon man in the hunt. He also had the benefit of that ever-widening gap between human and animal intelligence. Fire, for example, could be used to terrify and round up wild horses.*

◁ *Driven ibex, too, among the rocky gorges of Siberia, would escape, or try to, by leaping across a gap. Occasional finds of many shattered bones suggest that this may have been another way for Cro-Magnon man to hunt for food.*

as scrapers, knives, perforators and burins which could in turn be used to produce further items from bone, antler, ivory, wood or animal skins. The earliest industries which show the preponderance of blade tools occur over 35,000 years ago in south-west Asia and North Africa.

Who made these first Upper Palaeolithic blade tools is not known at present but modern man already existed in the area, as is known from the sites of Qafzeh and Skhul in Israel. With the development of the punch-blade technique and the consequent increase in man's cultural potential these first Cro-Magnons probably expanded into south-eastern Europe and neighbouring parts of Asia. The temporarily improved climate of Europe and western Asia between 40,000 and 30,000 years ago probably

Reconstruction of the head of a very early representative of modern man, Homo sapiens sapiens. *His skull was found in a cave on Mount Carmel, Israel.*

Below: *Bands of early modern men spread gradually into the country occupied by the Neanderthals, about 35,000 years ago.*

aided the early Cro-Magnons in penetrating what had previously been the domain of the Neanderthals, who had been well adapted to the glacier environment of the former ice age. The balance of the competition between Neanderthals and Cro-Magnons, which may have lasted several thousands of years, was tipped in favour of the Cro-Magnons, and by 30,000 years ago there were only Cro-Magnons left in Europe to face the returning ice-sheets. What exactly occurred in Europe between 40,000 and 30,000 years ago may never be certainly known; the evidence of archaeology favours the idea of at least some continuity between the Neanderthals and Cro-Magnons, whereas the evidence of the fossil remains themselves only emphasizes the gap between the two forms of *Homo sapiens.*

Archaeologists can recognize a considerable number of tool-making styles, each developed or adapted from something that went before, and each named from the cave or other site where the style was first found and identified. The Solutrean, for instance, which lasted for about 4,000 years from about 20,000 years ago, had a much more refined technique of 'pressure-flaking' which produced long thin laurel-leaf-shaped points, some at least of which were so delicate that they could never have been used as tools. Following the Solutrean, and perhaps evolved from it, was the Magdalenian (named after the cave of La Madeleine, in the Dordogne region of France), which lasted from about 16,000 years ago to the end of the last ice age in Europe, about 12,000 years ago. The Magdalenian was perhaps the summit of Cro-Magnon achievement, when the quality of craftsmanship produced the most beautiful bone, ivory and antler tools, and artistic expression reached the heights displayed in the caves of Lascaux and Altamira. In eastern Europe and Soviet Asia there were other industries such as the Gravettian and

Reconstructions based on two fossil skulls of Homo sapiens sapiens *show distinct differences. The man from Předmostí, Czechoslovakia* (top) *is more robust than the one from Cro-Magnon, France, which has a completely 'modern' profile.*

An oil lamp used by a Palaeolithic artist to light the walls of the cave at Lascaux.

Pavlovian (or Eastern Gravettian) which were characterized by long, narrow knife blades and which were associated with open camp-sites such as Dolní Věstonice in Czechoslovakia.

The Cro-Magnon way of life and death

Although one normally associates the Cro-Magnons with caves, in certain parts of Europe and Asia there were no caves available and the requirements of a nomadic life were such that open-air camps had to be used by bands of hunters. Some of these sites have been excavated, revealing a great deal about the culture and way of life of the Cro-Magnons which we could never have learnt from cave excavations alone. Man was beginning to utilize naturally-occurring minerals as well as the products of animals and plants. Fossils were being collected as curios or charms, and the usefulness of iron pyrites in the production of fire was probably appreciated. Coal was occasionally mined for fuel (as at a site in Poland), and clay was being moulded and fired to produce long-lasting sculptures.

Tanning skins and sewing them into clothes was probably women's work among the Cro-Magnons.

The men, as well as hunting, made the tools and weapons.

As population increased, inter-tribal clashes such as this, over hunting or territory, were bound to increase as well. But intercourse between different groups would also have been beneficial, leading to exchange of experience and ideas—and of women.

One site which suggests that the Cro-Magnons wore well-made clothes and jewellery is the cemetery of Sungir, about 200 km north-east of Moscow. There, about 22,000 years ago, two adults and two children were buried together with large numbers of objects carved from bone and ivory. The skeleton of an elderly man, found in 1964, was buried lying face upwards in a grave which was coated with red ochre. The ochre had also been sprinkled on his body, and this practice was so widespread among the Cro-Magnons that it seems to have had a special ritual significance — perhaps it was symbolic of blood, or the colour of living flesh. The Sungir man was covered in hundreds of beads made from mammoth ivory, and their arrangement in rows across his chest indicates that they once ran across a fur tunic. He was also buried wearing several bracelets and a head-band of mammoth ivory. At about the same time, two boys were also buried near by, head to head, in a similarly rich grave. This time the grave contained ivory jewellery, pierced teeth from arctic foxes, spears and knives made from mammoth tusks, and several bone batons — so-called 'bâtons de commandement'. Batons of this kind, made from antlers and drilled with a single hole, may have had some special significance to the Cro-Magnons. Similar examples of personal jewellery are known from sites on the French-Italian Riviera where the importance of the Mediterranean is reflected in the fact that shells and fish vertebrae were used to produce necklaces. (Mammoths and arctic foxes probably did not exist this far south in Europe, even during the last ice age.) The form of the clothing used by the Cro-Magnons can be reconstructed from burials such as Sungir, and also from the occasional evidence of clothing and headdresses on Palaeolithic carvings of men and women. It would appear that pelts of animals were sewn together into tunics not unlike the 'parkas'

129

Treatment of the sick and wounded would probably have been the responsibility of the old men, who had the widest knowledge and the longest experience.

The elders of the tribe, as in modern hunter-gatherer societies, were valued — it can be assumed — for their accumulated store of wisdom and experience, which they would pass on to the younger members of the tribe.

made by modern Eskimos. It is also possible that snowshoes and snow-boots were in use by the Cro-Magnons where conditions made them necessary.

Between 1925 and 1951 the site of Dolní Věstonice in Czechoslovakia produced remains of several Cro-Magnons who were buried near a hillside camp-site nearly 30,000 years ago. One of the skeletons was buried in a contracted position, covered by red ochre and mammoth bones. Another had been cremated and the skull-bones were ochred and buried separately. The burials were associated with a camp-site consisting of at least five huts. One of the oval huts was as large as 15 × 9 metres in floor area, and they were built within a supporting wall of mammoth tusks and bones dug into the ground. Inside the wall there must have been a number of wooden stakes drawn together and covered with animal skins. The skins were probably sewn together before being draped over the wooden poles, and were weighed down with some of the large bones, tusks and stones of the surrounding wall. Outside one hut was a workshop for the production of tools, weapons and other objects.

Evidence from within the huts suggests that the hearths they contained were used to produce figurines of humans and animals from a mixture of clay and bone, although one hearth was also equipped with a roasting-spit constructed from mammoth bones. Around the hearths were stone slabs which may have been used as seats or work-tables for moulding the clay. The floors of some of the huts were littered with parts of figurines and clay balls, some even bearing the fingerprints of the artists. In addition to the 'kiln' debris there was one of the earliest known musical instruments, a bone flute, and a number of strange female statuettes, known as Palaeolithic 'Venuses'.

These figurines have enlarged breasts, buttocks and stomachs and they have continued to fascinate and mystify archaeologists since they were first found at Cro-Magnon sites in the last century. Over a hundred 'Venuses' are known from sites of varying ages ranging from western Europe to Soviet Asia, and they were produced in materials as different as clay, ivory and limestone. They generally show the exaggerated physique already mentioned, and have little detail in the face or limbs, often having a pointed base without feet. This had led to the suggestion that they were used within huts and caves as charms or fertility symbols. They may have represented an ideal of beauty or fecundity, since some seem to be pregnant, and their physique bears some resemblance to modern Bushwomen who show the environmental adaptation called steatopygia, which is a tendency to store fat on the buttocks. This human parallel of the camel's hump may have evolved in Cro-Magnon women too, in order that they could continue to bear and suckle children when food was scarce (as during the winter months).

Further evidence of the ability of the Cro-Magnons to adapt to harsh environments comes from the site of Kostienki, in the valley of the river Don, nearly 250 km south-east of Moscow. Excavations

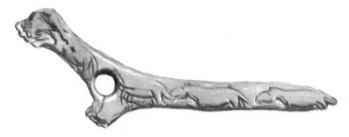

A bâton de commandement, *made from an antler and engraved with animal figures.*

Overleaf: *Encounters between tribes need not always have been aggressive. This picture (again based on what we know of modern tribal customs) shows an 'embassy' presenting gifts to the elders of a neighbouring tribe.*

The bâtons de commandement, *so often found in surroundings that suggest authority and power, may have been specially important symbols to the Cro-Magnons — perhaps as rewards for pre-eminent skill in the hunt.*

conducted from 1931 onwards show that the late Cro-Magnons who lived there perhaps 14,000 years ago were skilful hut-builders who had coped with life in a relatively treeless steppe environment by using bone, ivory and antler instead of wood for their implements, huts and even fuel. Their huts, which were long and narrow rather than oval, may have had double walls of furs or skins for extra insulation from the sub-zero winter temperatures outside. Inside the huts conditions must have been rather unpleasant — cramped (since several families probably shared each hut), smoky (since with the lack of wood it was necessary to burn bones and dung) and smelly (apart from the burning dung there was much refuse scattered inside them). Nevertheless as a winter shelter the huts were of great value and by this stage the Cro-Magnons had learnt to store dried and smoked meat, so the harsh winter months were not the times of hardship and starvation which they must have been for the Neanderthals and earliest Cro-Magnons. Having weathered the winter months, huge herds of mammoth, horse and saiga antelope were available so the Kostienki hunters could abandon their winter homes for another year, to follow the herds once again.

Tribes and totems

The increasingly efficient adaptations of the Cro-Magnons meant that the population density began to increase dramatically, with a corresponding increase in the frequency of contact between various tribes. This meant that new inventions and discoveries could be transmitted more easily from one group to the next across vast areas of Asia and Europe. Some of the encounters between groups were no doubt aggressive ones, as they would have been clashes over territory, or over herds to be hunted for food. But some meetings would probably have been more peaceful, with a real exchange of knowledge, and even of tribal members for the purpose of marriage. The tribal structures of the Cro-Magnons are, of course, unknown to us, but it can be guessed that by this stage their tribes were subdivided into sub-groups or clans which were governed by closer ties of family or blood relationship. It was probably forbidden to marry another member of the same clan,

A tribal magician foretelling success or failure in the hunt. Certain scenes in cave paintings, though difficult to interpret, may represent rituals such as this, which can be paralleled in primitive hunter-gatherer societies of today.

Among the wealth of finds
in a cave at Předmostí,
Czechoslovakia, is
a mammoth tusk on which
a Cro-Magnon artist
engraved a stylized 'Venus'
figure. Notice how the
figure—perhaps a fertility
symbol—has become reduced
almost to an abstraction,
with breasts, belly and
buttocks alone recognizable
as vestiges of the female.

Artistic achievement of a more formal, recognizable kind is
represented by models of animals, probably tribal totems,
made by east European contemporaries of the Cro-Magnons,
the Gravettians. This reconstruction is based on finds at the
site of Dolní Věstonice in Czechoslovakia.

One of the most famous paintings of prehistory, the so-called 'White Lady'. Found in a cave high up in South Africa's Drakensberg Mountains, it was painted by a Bushman artist some 9,000 years ago.

an extension of the taboo on mating within the family which seems almost universal among mankind. This 'incest' taboo led to the development of true exogamy, in which a woman would have to be won or exchanged from another clan or tribe. The more distant the other clan or tribe in degree of blood-relationship, the more likely they were to be hostile. But there were distinct advantages in such a system: it maintained physical diversity in each clan; it reduced hostility between groups as they gradually came to share more related individuals; and it helped to spread cultural innovations.

Each tribe or clan would have had its own special rules and perhaps even its own 'totem' — a specially revered animal, plant or object. The tribe or clan may even have been called by the name of its totem, and used the totem as its emblem (rather as a flag or badge is used today). If the totem was an animal such as a horse, then that animal was probably protected from hunting by the tribe in order that the tribe might remain healthy and enjoy successful hunting and food gathering. The tribe or clan may have believed that the totem animal was its ancient ancestor, or that dead members of the tribe were reincarnated as members of the totem species — hence to kill the totem animal would be to kill an ancestor. It is possible that some of the cave paintings depict totem animals, and that tribal members wore amulets carved with pictures of their totem animal during life and were buried with them at death.

We can only guess at the actual structure of clans and tribes which may have existed among the Cro-Magnons. There could have been a matrilineal or patrilineal system of descent, that is to say descent and group membership could have been traced

Necklaces such as these, made of shells and teeth, have been found at several Cro-Magnon sites. The craftsmen who made them (opposite) made their own tools: awls to drill the holes, scrapers and burins to engrave and decorate the 'beads'. These tools, too, have been found in quantity.

A beautifully painted bison on the walls of the Altamira cave, Spain, about 12,000 years old.

through females or males respectively. However, it is likely that men were the dominant powers in Cro-Magnon societies, as they generally are in most small-scale societies. There was probably a single chief, a figure respected for his intelligence, powers of leadership and hunting ability; it has been suggested that some of the richest Cro-Magnon burials were in fact those of chiefs. However, there are several examples of women and children being buried with rich grave goods, and women would no doubt have had an important role to play in social life beyond their roles as mothers, especially when the hunters were unsuccessful and the group had to rely on small game, plants and berries for food. We cannot know how much specialization of roles existed in Cro-Magnon societies, although there must surely have been a division of labour between men and women. But whether it was only the Cro-Magnon men who made tools and weapons and hunted large mammals, and only the women who made clothes, cooked and reared children is difficult to assess, particularly as we are viewing the Cro-Magnons through preconceived ideas derived from our own society.

As in many tribes today there were probably ceremonies which marked important events during an individual's life — puberty being one of the most obvious and significant. Even during Cro-Magnon times there were probably individuals who specialized in the direction of such activities and who acted as tribal shamans or magicians. These powerful individuals were believed to be able to communicate with the tribal totems or gods and were able to deliver messages from them. They were probably thought to have the ability to foretell the future, to influence the weather and the movements of herds of game, and to be able to cure diseases or inflict them on enemies. Certain scenes in cave paintings may depict ceremonies involving such tribal magicians.

A pregnant mare, painted on the walls of the Lascaux cave about 15,000 years ago.

This lifelike mammoth is engraved on a wall of the cave of Les Combarelles, France—an artistic creation all the more astonishing when we imagine the artist squatting, his tools at his side, in the flickeringly lit innermost recesses of the cave.

The 'Venus of Věstonice' was carved by a Palaeolithic artist about 25,000 years ago as a charm, or perhaps a fertility symbol.

Stylized simplicity: statuette of mammoth ivory found at Malta, Siberia.

A Palaeolithic artist carving a Venus statuette.

Art and magic

The Cro-Magnons were the earliest known artists. They portrayed a great variety of animals through their paintings and carvings on cave walls, and their work with stone, bone, antler and ivory. The mammoth tends to be the dominant animal represented by the Cro-Magnon artists of the open steppe-lands of eastern Europe and Soviet Asia, whereas horse, reindeer, bison and red deer predominate in the art of western Europe. People, plants and 'abstract' signs were also represented quite commonly, although the best work of the Cro-Magnons was reserved for the animals they hunted. Some of their art must have loomed large in the rituals of the Upper Palaeolithic peoples. The fact that it was often placed in inaccessible parts of caves indicates that it was not there to be easily admired as

143

Very rarely, Cro-Magnon sculptors produced carvings that seem to have been portraits rather than cult objects. The girl's head on the left was found at Brassempouy in the foothills of the Pyrenees, the boy's at Dolní Věstonice (Czechoslovakia).

A prehistoric artist with a sculptured 'Venus' in a Cro-Magnon encampment. The woman standing behind him suggests that he may have used a model; we cannot know, of course, but to carve such figurines without a model would need a high degree of creative sophistication.

Overleaf: *In the Lascaux cave. This supreme example of Cro-Magnon art, which has been called the Sistine Chapel of prehistory, dates back some 15,000 years.*

some sort of prehistoric art gallery. About 15,000 years ago, in the Tuc d'Audoubert cave in France, two clay bisons were modelled in perfect detail in an isolated chamber of the cave. Near by was a series of heel-prints, perhaps produced by several dancing children, and on the floor were a number of clay 'sausages'. In the neighbouring cave of Les Trois-Frères a remote, narrow passage flanked by carved and painted lions' heads led to a chamber with depictions of many strange hybrid animals. Some of these semi-human figures have been interpreted as the very shamans who controlled the rituals of Tuc d'Audoubert cave.

The real purpose behind Cro-Magnon art has intrigued archaeologists. For a long time the dominant theory was that of sympathetic magic. The Cro-Magnons represented animals they were going to hunt in order to exert some magical power over them.

Burials were probably accompanied by complex ceremonies and rites. Skeletons have been found which had clearly been buried with the limbs bound in a crouching position, and with tools and weapons arranged beside the body.

A tribal magician preparing for a ceremony in one of the caves—a possible explanation for the strange hybrid figures seen in some Cro-Magnon cave paintings.

Burial of a mammoth hunter (at Předmostí, Czechoslovakia).
Red ochre is being scattered over the body, which will then be
covered with a mammoth's shoulder blade.

Sometimes they drew the animals with wounds, or with spears piercing their bodies; in other cases some of the animals were painted dead or dying. Thus this theory suggests that cave art was produced to make the hunt successful. The site of Montespan in France contained a large headless clay statue of a bear with the skull of a bear-cub near by which had formerly been attached as the head of the model. As the statue was peppered with holes it seems probable that it had been used in some ritual concerned with hunting. Perhaps an actual bearskin had been draped over the statue, and young initiates had undergone a ceremony in which they had to stab it symbolically or throw spears at it.

A more recent and far-reaching theory proposed by the French archaeologist Leroi-Gourhan has built up a vast and detailed picture of Cro-Magnon religious beliefs. From a study of many caves and the paintings they contained, Leroi-Gourhan suggested that depictions of animals and signs represented sexual symbols, with male elements (e. g. deer, rhinoceros, bear, and signs such as points and barbs) located in peripheral parts of the caves, balanced by female elements (animals such as bison; signs such as ovals and triangles) concentrated in the centre of the cave system. The complex cosmological beliefs implied by Leroi-Gourhan's studies were certainly within the capabilities of the Cro-Magnons, as were the concepts suggested by the research of the American archaeologist, Marshack. Following a careful study of certain examples of cave art, sometimes using a microscope, he put forward the idea that the Cro-Magnons were using primitive calendars based on the changing seasons and the phases of the moon. Furthermore they had specific symbols for elements such as water, and represented times of the year by compositions of animals, plants and symbols appropriate to that season.

However, we should remember that Cro-Magnon art covers a period of 20,000 years, and we have

already remarked on the physical and cultural variety which existed during that period. So despite certain recurring elements in Cro-Magnon art, it seems

◁ *The burial of two Cro-Magnon children, side by side and wearing their jewelry. This reconstruction is based on a find at Menton on the French Riviera.*

An initiation ceremony in the Tuc d'Audoubert cave, France.

difficult to accept that there were relatively standard patterns in cave art which can be traced over vast distances and periods of time. Furthermore we must beware of looking at Cro-Magnon art through twentieth-century eyes, even if the eyes are those of psychologists or modern 'hunter-gatherers' who still produce their own 'cave art'.

Finds of *Homo sapiens sapiens* (modern man) from the Upper Palaeolithic

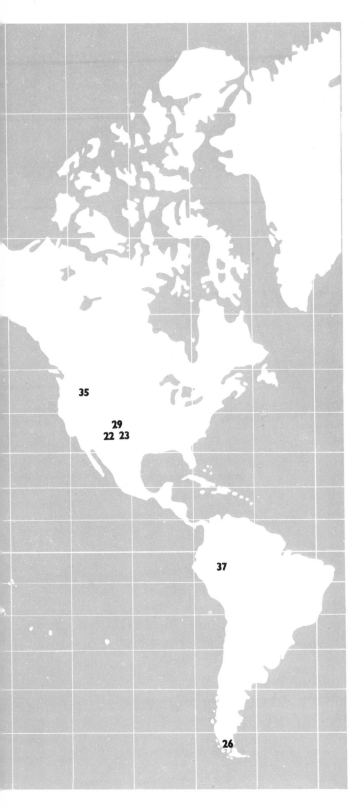

Key

1	Cro-Magnon, France	1866
2	Solutré, France	1866
3	Býčí Skála, Czechoslovakia	1871
4	Grimaldi-Menton, Italy	1872 – 1901
5	Chancelade, France	1888
6	Brno, Czechoslovakia	1885 – 91
7	Předmostí, Czechoslovakia	1894
8	Wadjak, Indonesia	1890 – 95
9	Combe-Capelle, France	1909
10	Boskop, S. Africa	1913
11	Oberkassel, W. Germany	1914
12	Podkumok, USSR	1918
13	Asselar, Mali	1927
14	Dolní Věstonice, Czechoslovakia	1925 – 49
15	Paviland, Wales	1822 – 1912
16	Afalou-bou-Rhummel, Algeria	1928 – 30
17	Malta, USSR	1931
18	Elmenteita, Kenya	1917 – 27
19	Afontova Gora, USSR	1923 – 37
20	Choukoutien, China	1930
21	Singa, Sudan	1924
22	Folsom, USA	1948 – 56
23	Sandia, USA	1949 – 52
24	Kostienki, USSR	1957 – 59
25	Niah, Sarawak	1958
26	Fell's Cave, Chile	1937
27	Ngandong, Indonesia	1965
28	Hoa-Binh, Vietnam	1965
29	Clovis, USA	1965 – 69
30	Fatima Koba, USSR	1969 – 70
31	Murzak Koba, USSR	1969 – 70
32	Olduvai, Tanzania	1970 – 75
33	Lake Mungo, Australia	1968 – 75
34	Arnhemland, Australia	1970 – 75
35	Lewisville, USA	1970 – 75
36	Amud, Israel	1974 – 75
37	El Inga, Ecuador	1974 – 75
38	Yukon, Alaska, USA	1974 – 75
39	Kota Tampan, Malaysia	1974 – 75
40	Soan, India	1975

7　Peopling the Earth

Today we have only a rough idea of whither and when groups of Palaeolithic people spread throughout the Old World. The only traces left behind are their stone implements, food waste, discarded remnants of hunting expeditions, remains of temporary dwellings and, occasionally, their own skeletons. Of these, the stone tools and weapons are by far the most abundant. They give a good indication of the level of skill reached by the people who made them and in various geographical areas the traditions can be traced back over long periods of time. New methods of tool-making probably took many generations to develop, although there would certainly have been opportunities to learn new techniques as small bands of Palaeolithic hunters met during their nomadic wanderings. However, the diffusion of new techniques and new ways of making things does not necessarily imply population movements. Ideas spread faster than the people who produce them. Therefore, although the distinctive styles of stone implements found in various parts of the world during the Upper Palaeolithic give some clues about the physical types of the people who made them (assuming that a close association can be established between important 'cultural centres' and human skeletal remains), for the most part we can do little more than guess at the size and composition of the populations who, during the last great ice age, were spreading through the tundra, steppes, forests and plains of the world.

In some ways this period was one of the most significant in the history of the human species. It was marked by the appearance, for the first time, of truly modern man, members of the sub-species *Homo sapiens sapiens* to which all the contemporary peoples of the world belong. Their physical characteristics

Tahitian girl, a member of the Polynesian geographical race. Her ancestors spread to the central Pacific from western Oceania in historical times.

were essentially similar to those of individuals in modern populations, with none of the extreme specializations of brow, braincase, face and physique possessed by earlier populations such as the Neanderthals. There is no way of telling what their external features such as skin colour and hair form were like (undoubtedly these would have varied from region to region) but there is no reason to believe that, appropriately dressed, they would have looked out of place in a multi-national crowd today.

As far as we can judge from the fossil record, these earliest representatives of modern man made their appearance around 40,000 years ago. The earliest example that we have on record is from the Niah cave in Borneo. Many others follow, dated between 40,000 and 30,000 years ago, in Europe, the Middle East, China, Indonesia and Australia.

Many theories have been advanced to explain the origin of modern man and the emergence of contemporary human 'races' but these tend to lean towards one or other of two extremes. One maintains that there was a single local centre of origin from which members of the sub-species *Homo sapiens sapiens* dispersed to colonize all the major continents. According to the other, the transition from earlier forms to modern man took place gradually in various parts of the world over a long period of time. There were many centres of origin and no widespread dispersal.

The first of these extreme views goes some way to explaining the rather sudden appearance in the fossil record of anatomically modern man alongside less advanced predecessors, the Neanderthals of Europe. The geographical location of the dispersal centre in which the final stages of evolution of modern man are supposed to have occurred has not been identified.

The second theory argues that the lines of descent leading to modern man (which, according to some research workers, can be traced as far back as the

Middle Pleistocene) all passed through a 'Neanderthal-like' phase which eventually gave way to forms of a more slender appearance with smaller skulls and faces. This happened when more efficient tools were developed and teeth were no longer needed for holding, chewing or biting materials during the manufacture of clothing, weapons and utensils or the preparation of food.

Whichever theory is correct — and the answer, if it is ever known, will probably lie in a blending of the two extremes — it is certain that by 40,000—35,000 years ago men of modern type were widely distributed throughout the Old World. For the most part it is difficult to say whether these early people resembled the present native inhabitants of the same geographical regions and whether or not they can be considered as part of the same ancestral stock. In a few cases, for example skulls from Europe, Indonesia and Australia, some resemblances can be detected but on the whole, at this time-depth, the connections with modern populations are not clear. Surprisingly enough, in Africa, the continent which is considered by some to be the cradle of human evolution and which has been populated (though on a very restricted scale) by members of the genus *Homo* for over three million years, the origins and distribution of peoples of modern type are very largely obscure. It is not until much later in the fossil record, about the beginning of the Neolithic period some 10,000 years ago, that recognizably 'modern' Africans can be identified from the skeletal remains.

An East Asian, with facial features characteristic of the Mongoloid geographical race.

After the ice ages

Before looking in detail at the characteristics of the major geographical groupings or 'races' of man today we shall examine some of the factors that have

 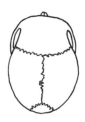 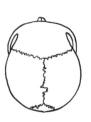

Skull shapes: long (dolichocephalic), medium (mesocephalic), broad (brachycephalic). This is an important characteristic of human variation but no longer used alone for classifying human races.

influenced the formation of distinctive physical features in human populations. The final chapter in the spread and differentiation of modern man occurred at a time of great climatic change. The cold glacial stages of the last ice age and the warmer interglacials were accompanied by advances and retreats of the ice in Europe, Asia and America and by periods of heavy rainfall interspersed with warmer, dry conditions closer to the equator. In the northern hemisphere the areas of land available for human settlement were at times very restricted. Ice sheets covered vast tracts of land and forced many of the animals and the men who hunted them further south.

During this phase of nomadic existence the hunters and food-gatherers of the Upper Palaeolithic were subjected to a very wide range of environmental conditions. Their technology was primitive. They had some form of clothing, simple utensils, crude shelters, and fire, but the extent to which they could change their local environment was very limited. By comparison with even the least well equipped modern human populations they would have been extremely vulnerable to the elements. In order to survive they had to adapt. Over many generations and several thousand years the process of adaptation led to the formation of distinctive physical and genetic characteristics. Populations, often small in size, developed further differences as a result of geographical isolation and splitting into smaller migratory groups. Much of the remarkable diversity in our species today has its roots in the changing and sometimes harsh conditions of the last ice age.

Certain biological rules that deal with adaptations to climate in animals can, to some extent, be applied to man. The same forces of natural selection operate to produce characteristics that increase the chances of survival in a particular environment. For example, long, lean bodies with large surface areas for efficient heat loss are found in warm, humid conditions. Further north, as temperatures drop, bodies become more spherical or stocky in shape and limbs shorten — a more efficient form for heat conservation. Skin colour is also related to climate and latitude, skins with greater amounts of the brownish-black pigment melanin being found in regions of high solar radiation where intense ultra-violet light causes severe burns and cancers in unprotected fair skins. Nostril shape, hair form and eye colour may also be related to climatic conditions although the evidence is not altogether conclusive.

Climate and colour

It is probable that human skin colour was originally brown, combining the protective qualities of melanin, needed in the tropical habitats occupied by the early hominids, with some reflective properties that minimized the amount of radiant heat absorbed (this would have been specially important during hunting expeditions in open country). As human populations spread to higher latitudes, where sunlight was less intense and cloud cover more extensive, there was a tendency for natural selection to favour a lighter skin colour. This allowed more vitamin D to be produced beneath the skin by the action of ultra-violet light. This vitamin is important for healthy bone development, and when foods containing dietary vitamin D are not plentiful the body must be able to make it in the inner layers of the skin.

As skin colour is one of the most conspicuous characteristics of human variation it is not surprising that it has been used to classify human populations into different 'races'. However, such classifications have given a very misleading impression of the actual biological relationships between various geographical population groups. Nowadays the principal characteristics used to classify populations or to study their affinities include external features such as head and face shape, hair form and colour, eye form, skin colour, body build and fingerprint patterns. Then there are many internal characteristics such as blood groups, blood proteins, taste-sensitivity and colour-blindness. Most people are aware of their ABO and Rhesus blood groups but today samples of blood are often tested routinely for over 30 groups and systems. The frequencies of these inherited blood factors are extremely useful as they give a good idea of the closeness or otherwise of relationship between various population groups.

A central European. The Caucasoid race to which he belongs accounts for over fifty per cent of the world population.

What is 'race'?

Most anthropologists now agree that some sort of classification for the major geographical populations of man is useful, although opinions are still divided on whether the human species can be classified into true biological races and, if so, how many can be identified.

An East African 'Negroid'. The origins of the most recent branch of this geographical race are still largely obscure.

Opposite above: *The Tasmanian woman Truganina, the last survivor of an ancient Australoid population which was brought to extinction in the last quarter of the nineteenth century.*

Opposite below: *William Lanney, a Tasmanian, whose death in 1869 preceded that of his wife, Truganina, by seven years. Facial features of the Tasmanians differed in several notable respects from the aborigines of mainland Australia.*

A 'race' has been defined as a subdivision of a species formed by a group of individuals sharing certain biological characteristics that distinguish them from all other groups. These biological characteristics are often linked with cultural characteristics that are also shared by members of the group. One system of classification that is frequently used subdivides human populations into four main groupings. These are the Mongoloids, which include most of the native inhabitants of central, east and south-east Asia and the Americas; Caucasoids, which include the peoples of Europe, the Middle East, India and North Africa; the Negroids of Africa; and the Australoids, aboriginal inhabitants of Australia, New Guinea, island Melanesia and isolated areas of Indonesia. Populations such as the Polynesians, Micronesians, the Veddas of Sri Lanka and the Ainu of northern Japan do not fit well into this scheme but in general it separates the main populations of man into a small number of biologically meaningful races, each of which has a set of reasonably well-defined characteristics.

The Mongoloids

The Mongoloids probably originated in north-eastern Asia from a general and very varied Upper Palaeolithic population represented by the Upper Cave people of Choukoutien, China. These 'proto-Mongoloid' peoples were ancestors not only of later so-called 'classical Mongoloids' but also, as we shall see, of the American Indians.

Typical characteristics of the 'classical Mongoloids' include yellowish skin; coarse, straight black hair; little beard or body hair; a flat face and nose; eyes with 'epicanthic folds'; high, flared cheekbones; and front teeth with a scooped-out appearance from behind, called 'shovel-shaped incisors'. The formation of these 'classical Mongoloid' features was probably the outcome of isolation and adaptation during the intensely cold conditions of the last glaciation.

Although skulls dated to the last glacial period in China show more recognizable Mongoloid characters it is not until the Neolithic period that skulls have been found that are similar in most respects to those of modern Chinese. According to one theory the Mongoloid population of East Asia increased very rapidly at the end of the last ice age. During the Neolithic period farmers from the west, of a different racial type, migrated into China and introduced agricultural techniques to the nomadic Mongoloid tribesmen. This was followed by a southward expansion of the now slightly mixed population through Indochina, Thailand and Burma and eventually to Indonesia. At a later date warriors from Mongolia crossed the plains of western Asia on horseback to invade the territory of the Caucasoids. The Turks and Tatars gathered followers from among the western nomads and invaded north-east Europe and the eastern Baltic. Their influence can still be seen in the physical types of the present-day speakers of Finno-Ugrian languages, in Finland, Estonia and Hungary.

There is no clearly defined boundary between races in western Asia, neither is there in the south-east, where Mongoloids merged in prehistoric times with the ancestors of the Melanesians, Australians and Pacific islanders to form the present Indonesian-Malay groups. Only in the south has the barrier of the Himalayas made a reasonably sharp division between the Mongoloids of the northern plateaux and the Caucasoids of the Indian lowlands.

TRUGANINA - (Lalla Rookh) † 1876

The Caucasoids

The name 'Caucasoid' was first used in the eighteenth century to describe the peoples of the Caucasus region between the Black Sea and the Caspian. The area was thought to be the original homeland of many of the populations of Europe and this is probably why the name 'Caucasoid' or 'Caucasian' has acquired a much broader usage. It includes not only the 'white' populations of Europe but also the peoples of the Middle East, India, north and east Africa (as far as Ethiopia and the Somali Republic). Today Caucasoid peoples constitute over 50 per cent of the total world population, compared with about 40 per cent for the Mongoloids and only 7 per cent for the Negroids.

The main distinguishing physical characteristics of Caucasoids are the high forehead, straight face, narrow and prominent nose, thin lips, well-developed chin and rather plentiful face and body hair. Such a variety of climate and environment is found in the Caucasoid domain that it is not surprising to find a wide variety of physical characteristics among members of this race. Some of them, for example pale complexions, are probably the result of adaptation to

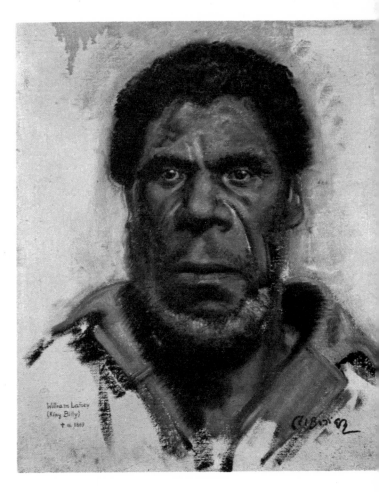

William Laney (King Billy) † 1869

cooler, cloudy conditions in high latitudes. In north-western Europe fair skins are associated with a high incidence of blond hair and blue eyes. This is in marked contrast to the dark skins and brownish-black hair of Caucasoids in north-east Africa and southern India.

In Europe the earliest skulls of a completely modern type come from the French site of Combe Capelle. The somewhat later but particularly well-known Cro-Magnon people were mostly tall and long-headed with rather short, broad faces. They were similar to the Upper Palaeolithic people of North Africa. It is impossible to identify the racial components of these early populations in present-day Europeans but it has been suggested that the Berbers of North Africa retain some of the characteristics of early Neolithic peoples who inhabited the same regions about 10,000 years ago.

The spread of the Caucasoids occurred after the European ice-sheets and glaciers had retreated. The warmer climate encouraged the growth of dense forests in the lowland regions but the herds of wild game preferred the more open tundra and tended to move northwards in the wake of the retreating ice. Groups of Neolithic hunters followed and eventually settled in the previously uninhabited areas of north-west Europe.

The spread of Caucasoid populations in north and north-west Africa had far-reaching effects. In Africa these populations participated in the blending of ethnic groups in Egypt, Ethiopia and Somaliland, in areas south of the Sahara and in the Sahara itself. The ancient Egyptians, who were responsible for one of the greatest civilizations of Africa, may have originated in western Asia. Skeletal evidence suggests that they were present in east Africa before the end of the Pleistocene and in advance of the arrival of the Negroids.

In India the pattern of settlement of the original Caucasoid migrants is difficult to reconstruct. There is a tremendous diversity of languages and physical types among the present inhabitants but three main groups can be distinguished. The darker-skinned population of southern India, speakers of the Dravidian group of languages, constitute one branch of the Caucasoids. The second, by far the largest, comprises the lighter-skinned, lightly built 'Mediterranean' Caucasoids, speakers of Indo-European (Aryan) languages. The third type, sometimes referred to as 'Veddoid', includes many of the dark-skinned aboriginal populations of central and southern India, whose affinities probably lie with the early 'proto-Australoid' peoples of south-east Asia and the Pacific.

The Australoids

The Australoids probably originated from a late Pleistocene population centred in southern Asia, which spread southwards to occupy a large area of land called 'Sundaland', much of which is now beneath the sea. It included the whole of present south-east Asia, Sumatra, Java and Borneo and its boundary is now marked by the sub-oceanic Sunda Shelf. The Philippines and Celebes were part of larger land masses but, with Sundaland, were separated from another large continent, 'Sahulland' (which included present Australia, Tasmania and New Guinea) by a deep-water channel just to the west of Timor and Ceram. This was the water barrier (known as the Wallace Line, after Charles Darwin's friend and collaborator, Alfred Russel Wallace) which isolated the primitive mammals of Australia and New Guinea from the more advanced mammals of south-east Asia. It was also the barrier that the ancestors of Melanesians and Australians had to negotiate to reach Sahulland around 30,000 years ago.

The pattern of settlement of Australia is not easy to determine from the limited archaeological evidence but the distribution of sites suggests that the first areas to be inhabited may have been in the narrow coastal strip to the east and the well-watered areas of the south-east, including Tasmania. The less promising grasslands in the west and interior of the continent were probably settled later and the central Australian deserts may not have been inhabited until recent historical times.

The earliest remains of man in Australia come from Lake Mungo in the south-east. They are

Australoids, men of central Australia whose remarkable culture and ability to survive in a hostile environment reflect the way of life of Mesolithic hunters and gatherers.

unquestionably of modern type though a little more robust in skull shape than modern Australian aboriginals. The first settlers carried with them a simple tool-kit of stone implements which persisted everywhere without much change for most of prehistoric time. Only at the end of the Pleistocene, when Tasmania was severed from the mainland by rising seas (about 12,500 years ago), were new ideas of stone-working introduced. The dingo made its first appearance at this time. The men themselves seem to have been of two types, one resembling some of the present inhabitants of New Guinea, island Melanesia and the known Tasmanians, the other being of a more robust type with low, flattened foreheads and large faces. Some anthropologists see in the second type a resemblance to the Upper Pleistocene population of Java.

When Australia was first discovered by the Europeans its dark-skinned inhabitants numbered between three hundred thousand and half a million. From the end of the eighteenth century, however, these aboriginal hunters and gatherers were gradually forced back into less fertile regions where game was more scarce. As a result, numbers dwindled and today there are no more than about 40,000 full-blooded aborigines and about the same number of mixed-blooded individuals (the product of Australoid-Caucasoid mixture).

The physical characteristics of the mainland aborigines are surprisingly varied, with hair ranging from straight to frizzy in form and from dark brown to tawny (especially among young children of central Australia) in colour. Skin runs from warm chocolate brown to very dark. Body build tends to be more slender than in Europeans, with characteristically long legs and arms. The most striking features are those of the head and face: prominent brows, deepset eyes, broad noses with a depressed nasal root, and large mouths.

According to the disappointingly small number of observations recorded by European explorers and colonists and a few photographs, the aborigines of

Melanesians: tribal dancers of Papua New Guinea, richly adorned with bird-of-paradise plumes. Their distant ancestors settled in the mountainous interior of the island over 30,000 years ago, while another branch of the Australoids continued to Australia.

Tasmania were noticeably different from those of the mainland. Skins were darker, hair was more tightly curled, faces shorter and skulls broader. The last of the Tasmanians died in 1876, a tragic event in the history of the human races that would never have happened but for the brutal treatment, the effects of disease and the destruction of traditional hunting grounds suffered by the whole population at the hands of the European colonists.

The unique way of life of the present aboriginal Australians gives a valuable insight into human prehistory. Probably no other living population is closer to the primitive hunter-gatherer state of our Palaeolithic ancestors. The adaptation of the aborigines to the largely inhospitable conditions and harsh environment of the Australian outback is remarkable. When European colonists first arrived they found a land inhabited by people using implements and weapons made only of wood, stone and bone. These people had no bow and arrow although they did possess some very efficient hand-thrown weapons, including a variety of throwing clubs and the famous boomerang (intended to fly straight and do great damage to enemy or prey — the returning type is a toy). Spears were sped with greater force by an ingenious holder known as the woomera. Stone tools were often made by a simple flaking technique although some axes were edge-ground and hafted to handles.

The Australians lived almost entirely on wild edible plants and small animals, occasionally catching game and fish. They inhabited open woodlands or semi-desert regions and each tribe had its own territory, over which it constantly moved about. The men tracked game (mostly kangaroos and other marsupials) and the women gathered edible parts of fruits, tubers and leaves, birds' eggs and grubs. They never remained long in one place, they had no knowledge of farming and their only domestic animal was the dingo. Like prehistoric hunters they were excellent trackers, bird-hunters and fishermen. They could make fires using wooden 'drilling sticks' and dried grass and could find underground sources of water in places where civilized man would require modern equipment and techniques.

The Tasmanians, until their extinction in the second half of the nineteenth century, represented one of the most isolated ethnic groups in the world.

They had a very primitive array of stone implements and unlike the mainland aborigines had no knowledge of the spear-thrower or the boomerang. The dingo was unknown to them and although they lived on an island with accessible seashores they appear to have lived mainly by hunting small animals and gathering plants and molluscs. During early settlement times they may have been capable fishermen but by the time the Europeans arrived practically all interest in fishing had been lost.

When the first British colonists came to Hobart in 1803 there were still about three to five thousand natives in existence. Harsh treatment by the white settlers and outright warfare reduced their numbers very rapidly. The Europeans also brought with them diseases to which the aborigines had little resistance and this had a further effect on the size of the population. In 1842 the 300 or so men, women and children who remained were evacuated to islands in the Bass Strait (including Flinders Island) largely through the efforts of a well-meaning Englishman, G. A. Robinson, and an energetic young aboriginal woman, Truganina, both of whom were appalled at the brutal treatment suffered by the native people. There, deprived of their traditional way of life, they became so thoroughly demoralized that many of them lost the will to live. Truganina was the last survivor, dying a forlorn old woman in Hobart in 1876.

The Pacific islanders

The aborigines of New Guinea, the second largest island in the world, are Melanesians, although this term is sometimes restricted to the natives of the coast and islands, the name 'Papuan' being reserved for the inhabitants of the interior. This subdivision is rather artificial although there are some grounds for looking upon the Papuans as the distant ancestors of the earliest settlers of the island. Their physical characteristics are somewhat distinct, the Papuans having a stockier, more muscular physique, longer, lower heads and more rugged-looking faces than the peoples of the coast, who have been subject to much greater population movements and contact with islanders to the north and east, many of whom were later arrivals in the area. Papuans have a number of physical features that are similar to those of Australian aborigines, with whom they share a common ancestry. Brows are prominent, noses broad (sometimes with a 'hooked' appearance), eyes are deep-set. Skins are dark but very variable, hair ranges from tightly coiled to the frizzy condition that gave rise to the affectionate term 'Fuzzy-wuzzy', used by the Australian and American troops of their Papuan colleagues-at-arms during the Pacific war.

◁ *Dancers of the Marquesas Islands welcoming the spring. Their homeland was a centre for Polynesian migrations about 2000 years ago.*

New Zealand Maori with face carving. The North and South Islands were settled by Polynesians in about AD 500.

Stature is a little lower than in Australian aborigines, averaging about 160 cm (5ft 3in.) in men.

The earliest evidence of occupation comes from an open site in the central Papuan highlands where stone tools have been dated to about 26,000 years ago. The distant ancestors of the present Papua New Guineans represented one branch of migrants from south-east Asia (Sundaland) who remained in New Guinea while others crossed the then dry land of the Torres Strait on the Sahul shelf to reach Australia. The interior of the island is very mountainous, with deep valleys covered in many parts by dense tropical rain-forest. During the course of settlement and until recent times small populations have been isolated from one another by these formidable geographical barriers, with only occasional contact between them. As a result, not only a great variety of physical and genetical characteristics can now be found among the peoples of New Guinea but also a bewildering diversity of languages. There are over 500 in the highlands of the former Australian-administered Territory of Papua New Guinea alone.

Unlike the Australians, the Papuans learned the fundamentals of tropical agriculture, the domestication of animals and the arts of fishing and navigation through the diffusion of knowledge and people from Indonesia. The process started in about 4000 BC and continued until historical times. There is a sharp division of labour between members of the communities, hunting and building being the province of the men while the agricultural work is done mainly by the women. Staple food crops vary from region to region but consist mainly of yams, taros and sweet potatoes, bananas and greens. Meat is eaten rarely and then principally on ceremonial occasions such as weddings or burial feasts. Ceremonies are accompanied by elaborate ritual and include chanting and dancing on a grand scale with participants adorned in superb ornaments and head-dresses of bird of paradise plumes.

The Polynesian islands lie inside a triangular area of the Pacific, each side of which measures about 5000 miles. Hawaii is at the top, Samoa and Tonga halfway down on the western side, with New Zealand at the bottom. Tahiti lies in the centre and Easter Island marks the point furthest to the east. In view of the skilled navigation needed to cover the immense distances between many of the islands, it is not surprising that Polynesia was populated only at a relatively late date.

A number of theories have been advanced to explain Polynesian origins including the one proposed by Thor Heyerdahl after his epic voyage in the *Kon Tiki,* when he suggested that some of the original migration of peoples had been from America. Most anthropologists now consider that an earlier theory of south-east Asian origin is essentially correct. Archaeological, anthropological and language studies support this view. It appears that from about 4500 years ago there was a parent colony of Polynesian-like people in the Caroline Islands of Micronesia. As the population grew, dispersals took place in every direction. By about 3500 years ago people had filtered into the central western side of the Polynesian triangle. There, over the next thousand years, they acquired pigs, chickens, dogs and plants from their Melanesian neighbours. The main dispersals to the east took place about 1700 years ago (i. e. about AD 300) from a centre probably located in the Marquesas Islands. Polynesians in large twin-hulled canoes, some as much as 100 ft long, carrying 140 men, voyaged northwards to Hawaii, eastwards to Easter Island and south-westwards to the Society and Cook Islands and New Zealand.

Polynesians are often noted for their good looks and well-proportioned bodies. In fact it is very difficult to generalize about their physical features for, as a result of their composite origin, they are very variable. Some of the Polynesians show Mongoloid features which resemble the present inhabitants of Indonesia and Malaysia. Others are more 'Australoid' in appearance, like the Melanesians.

The Maoris are thought to be the descendants of the earliest colonizers of Polynesia although their arrivals in the North and South Islands of New Zealand almost certainly occurred during the period AD 500—900. According to Polynesian tradition these people bear the name given by the original inhabitants of Polynesia to their forefathers. The Maoris retained many of the characteristics of the life

Mbuti pygmies, the smallest people in the world, are well adapted for moving silently about the equatorial rain-forest of Central Africa.

and culture of Old Polynesia, such as the art of wood-carving, artistic tattooing, a knowledge of navigation and a tradition of ancient legends and myths.

Before the arrival of Europeans and people of other nationalities most of the original inhabitants of Oceania had reached a late Neolithic or even higher cultural level. The most recent is the Malayan-Polynesian culture, which reached Oceania at the beginning of the historical era via the Philippines and Indonesia. It was characterized by a relatively highly developed social system, an advanced religion and hierarchy, accompanied by ceremonies and ritual dances, and a hereditary system of rulers and gods. Many of these features have been preserved to the present day.

The varied peoples of Africa

Settlement of Africa took a good deal longer than the other major continents. Up to the end of the Palaeolithic the tropical rain-forests and network of rivers in the interior virtually ruled out settlement of the central and western parts. Towards the end of the

Caucasoid territory in the north and east. It includes not only the large Bantu-speaking and West African groups and the East African Nilotes but also the Khoisan peoples (Bushmen and Hottentots) and the Negrillos (pygmies). Attempts at defining the physical characteristics of Negroids are never very satisfactory but in general they are characterized by narrow heads, rounded foreheads, prognathism (protruding mid-facial region), broad noses, thick lips, slender limbs, dark skins, woolly hair and sparse beard and body hair.

Some of the earliest fossil skulls to have recognizably Negroid characteristics have been found in South Africa together with stone tools of a Middle Palaeolithic type. Some anthropologists believe that these represent ancestors of the modern Hottentots and Bushmen, known collectively as the Khoisan. (The term is made up of two words, *Khoikoi*, the Hottentots' name for themselves, and *San*, their name for the Bushmen.) Whether or not this can be shown to be correct, it is clear that the ancestors of the Khoisan peoples once inhabited a much wider territory but are now confined to a few relatively inhospitable areas into which they retreated before the invading Bantu negroes coming from the north in Iron Age times.

Of a total of about 55,000 Bushmen, most are distributed in the Kalahari Desert, some live in the Okavango Swamp and others in more heavily wooded areas such as southern Angola. Traditionally they are nomadic hunters and gatherers, with weapons and implements not very different from those used by their ancestors over 10,000 years ago. Hunting is done by bow and poisoned arrows, throwing sticks and spears. The women use pointed digging sticks to obtain roots and tubers. Their living shelters are simple dome-shaped constructions made of branches and they have few possessions.

Average stature of the Bushmen is about 157 cm (5 ft 2 in.). Their yellowish-brown skin colour is a good deal lighter than many African populations and the skin itself is often very wrinkled. The face is short and small with prominent cheekbones and

Pleistocene there is some evidence that a drop in temperature occurred and with it changes in vegetation which may have made some regions more accessible to man. From the time of appearance of the earliest human populations the most favourable conditions were found in the open northern part of the continent bordering the Mediterranean, the eastern part, including the Great Rift Valley and lakes, and the tropical south and south-west.

The people of Africa are so varied that the term 'Negroid' is scarcely adequate to describe all the dark-skinned populations south of the predominantly

Bantu chieftain of the Zulu tribe of southern Africa. Superior weapons and agricultural techniques made possible a great Iron Age expansion of the Bantu populations in the third and fourth centuries AD.

Negroid: a Kikuyu woman of Kenya.

a pointed chin. Eyes are narrow and sometimes have a fold across the middle of the eyelid which appears to serve as a protection against the glare of the sun. The hair is so tightly spiralled that it forms small 'peppercorn' tufts separated by bare patches on the scalp. The ear is rather square in shape and the lobe is often absent. One of the most conspicuous characteristics that occurs in Bushman and Hottentot women is a fatty accumulation on the buttocks and thighs known as 'steatopygia'. It may serve as a food store for the body during periods of drought but ancient cave paintings show women with steatopygia at times when the Khoisan were living in relatively fertile, well-watered territory, so this argument may not be altogether correct. The fact that the condition is much admired by the men indicates that sexual selection may also have played a part in preserving this interesting characteristic.

Hottentots are pastoralists, keeping herds of long-horned cattle, fat-tailed sheep and goats. They number about 30,000 in southern and south-western Africa and only two groups still retain their ethnic individuality, the Nama and the near-extinct Korana. Inter-marriage between early Dutch settlers and Hottentot women produced the Reheboth people of South Africa, while the so-called Cape Coloured population resulted from the mixing of Khoisan, Bantu, Asian and European ingredients.

The Bantu-speaking peoples, who with the Europeans were responsible for forcing the Khoisan groups into their present harsh environments and reducing their numbers, are the largest of the African population groups. About 70 million people speak the Bantu languages and the area they occupy extends south of a line from Duala on the Atlantic coast to the mouth of the Tana River on the Indian Ocean, covering much of southern Africa. West Africa is traditionally viewed as their homeland but there is not much skeletal material, perhaps because the humid environment is not suitable for good preservation of bone. It is not until a time-level of about 10,000 years ago that skulls with a definite Negro appearance occur in the fossil record.

Language studies indicate that eastern Nigeria may have been the original homeland of the Bantu and that at some relatively recent period of African prehistory Bantu-speakers migrated across the equatorial rain-forest to a central area roughly on a level with the mouth of the Congo River. This eventually formed a nucleus for a great expansion of the Bantu population during the Iron Age, about the third and fourth centuries AD. Superior methods of exploiting the environment by the use of iron implements and weapons, together with a good knowledge of agricultural techniques, paved the way for the rapid increase in population numbers.

The Nilotes live in the White Nile region of southern Sudan. They belong to three main population groups, the Nuer, the Dinka and the Shilluk. They are characterized by very distinctive physical and genetic characteristics which set them apart from all other African populations, the most notable being their extremely slender and elongated body build. The Nuer have the highest recorded stature for any population in the world — 185 cm (6ft 1in.) in a small sample of men. The other groups are also very tall, averaging about 175 cm (5ft 10in.). The Nuer and Dinka are primarily cattle herdsmen but they supplement their diet of meat by cultivating millet and spearing fish. They move their herds to riverside pastures during the dry season and back to more permanent settlements on higher ground during the rains. The Shilluk stay in permanent communities, depending more on agricultural produce and fish for their subsistence than on their cattle.

Although the broad noses, full lips and prominent lower faces of the Nilotes are similar to other Negroids, their heads are outstandingly long and narrow and their skins extremely dark. Their slender body build is a great advantage in the hot, dry environment of the Sudan and is probably the result of natural selection during a long period of adaptation to exceptional environmental conditions. Unfortunately the fossil record has shed very little light on their origins.

Of all the peoples of mankind the pygmies of Africa deserve special mention. They are of great interest not only because of their small size but also because they represent the survivors of an ancient Negroid population who have retained many elements of a Mesolithic hunter-gatherer way of life and have lived for a long time in their present habitat.

The only true pygmies, the Mbuti, inhabit the Ituri forest, the north-eastern corner of the equatorial forest of central Africa. They number about 40,000 and live in semi-nomadic bands, hunting wild pigs, antelopes, monkeys, apes and even elephants as well as a variety of small animals. Mbuti women collect wild fruits and roots, lizards, shellfish and insects. The tribes keep no domestic animals other than the dog and practise no agriculture.

It is difficult to say how long the ancestors of the Mbuti have lived in the tropical forest. Perhaps because of the poor conditions for preservation, no fossil skeleton of a pygmy has yet been discovered. Evidence for their antiquity rests on the discovery of stone implements, the oldest of which are dated to about 20,000 years ago.

The stature of Mbuti men averages about 144 cm (4ft 9in.) and of the women about 137 cm (4ft 6in.). They have large heads relative to total body size, very broad noses and wide mouths. The middle part of the face is prominent. Compared with other African

populations their legs are relatively short but their shoulders are broad and their arms long. They are superbly adapted for living in the forest and have tremendous speed and agility when moving about the dense undergrowth. At one time it was thought that their small stature might be due to an inherited deficiency in growth hormone but it now appears that the action of normal levels of growth hormone is blocked in the body cells and tissues. Natural selection appears to have favoured small stature in the forest environment and once the genetic mechanism appeared in the ancestral Negroid stock it was perpetuated.

The first Americans

The ancestors of the American Indians probably crossed the ice-free land 'bridge' between eastern Siberia and Alaska about 25,000 years ago when the sea-levels of the last ice age were as much as 150 ft lower than they are today. A large area of land, known as Beringia, was exposed and this was accessible for most of the time to 'proto-Mongoloid' and early Mongoloid peoples of north-east Asia. Almost certainly these Palaeolithic hunters would have been drawn into this region by the opportunities it presented for tracking large herds of migrating caribou and other big game animals. The Beringian land-bridge had accumulated the natural fertilizers of the sea: marine animal and plant remains. The lush vegetation that grew there attracted the animals in large numbers. At the time when men are presumed to have first travelled across Beringia their passage to the east would have been blocked by glaciers. However, when sea levels rose with warmer temperatures, an ice-free corridor opened up between the Cordilleran and Laurentide ice-sheets, east of the Canadian Rockies. Slowly, the bands of big-game hunters would have been able to make their way through the watershed of the Mackenzie River towards the plains of North America.

Few traces of these first Americans have been found. Stones that look as though they have been worked by man for use as tools about 20,000 to 25,000 years ago have been found in New Mexico and Texas and the skull of Los Angeles man, discovered in 1936 by workmen digging a storm drain, has been given a date of about 23,600 years ago. Stone tools

Nilote from the southern Sudan carrying a shot pelican. His tall, slender physique is a tribal characteristic, and an evolutionary advantage in the fierce Sudanese heat.

perhaps 20,000 years old have been found in South
America, indicating that man had penetrated the
jungle area of Central America at an early date.

The first clear evidence of the way of life of
ancestral Americans does not appear until
a time-level of about 11,000 to 12,000 years, when the
skilful makers of fluted stone weapons, the Clovis and
Folsom spear points, were hunting game on the
plains of North America.

In South America some important finds have been
made at Fell's Cave in Tierra del Fuego, the

*A North American Indian
(Iroquois) of the Atlantic
coast. His distant
Mongoloid ancestors crossed
the Bering land-bridge from
Asia about 25,000 years
ago.*

*Tribal totem of Pacific
Indians (Haida).*

southernmost tip of the continent, where stone implements about 10,000 years old have been discovered. It is possible that at this time large areas of the Amazon basin, the forests and tablelands of the Gran Chaco and the plains of Patagonia were largely uninhabited and settlement took place mainly in the Neolithic period.

The physical appearance of many North American Indians is not as obviously Mongoloid as might be expected, in view of their east Asian ancestry. The hooked nose, coppery-coloured skin and absence of a complete epicanthic eye-fold sets them apart from the modern inhabitants of north-east Asia. However, these characteristics are by no means typical of the New World as a whole and the agricultural tribes of South America have in their facial features unmistakable traces of their Mongoloid ancestry.

The short, stocky Pueblo Indians are also typically Mongoloid. They come from the south-western part of North America and their culture is very well

known. These people and their ancestors have been agriculturalists for thousands of years and are noted for their skills in basket-making, a tradition that dates back to almost 2000 years ago. The word *pueblo* means 'village' and during the so-called Pueblo period hundreds of villages were built. The people were at one time driven into caves and elaborately constructed pit-dwellings by the invading nomads of the Great Gulf.

The Eskimos are relatively recent immigrants to the New World. It was not until about 4000 years ago that the Eskimos and their relatives the Aleuts arrived on the coast of western Alaska from Siberia. Evidence for this comes from stone tools, none of which pre-date this period, and from their languages, which are closer to those of the eastern side of the Bering Sea than to any spoken by the American Indians. The Bering land-bridge would have been submerged when the first Eskimos set out for America, so they must have arrived by boat or on foot by a perilous route across the pack-ice.

From Alaska the earliest Eskimos, skilled hunters of whales, seals and other marine mammals, spread across north-western Canada about 3000 years ago, on to the foggy banks of the Hudson Bay and from there to Baffin Island and Greenland. The groups that reached Newfoundland about 500 years later (the Dorset people) may have been the first American natives to have met Europeans — Viking explorers of 'Vinland'.

Not surprisingly, the whole pattern of life of the Eskimos has been greatly influenced by the harsh environment which they have mastered so courageously and successfully. One of the most valuable pieces of equipment that they brought with them to the Americas was the skin boat or 'kayak'. They also developed an astonishing array of special tools and devices to cope with virtually every demand of polar living. These included spears with throwers, harpoons, knives, scrapers, traps, lures, sledges and snowshoes. The famous igloo, which two people can build to family size in one or two hours, and the insulated pit-dwelling enable the Eskimos to live comfortably when outside temperatures are down to —40° C. Their physical characteristics and physiology as well as their unique culture are beautifully in tune with their environment.

Eskimos of the far North. These Mongoloids are among the most recent populations to disperse and settle during the global spread of human races. Their fine cultural innovations have enabled them to conquer some of the world's most inhospitable regions.

Life-patterns of early man round the world

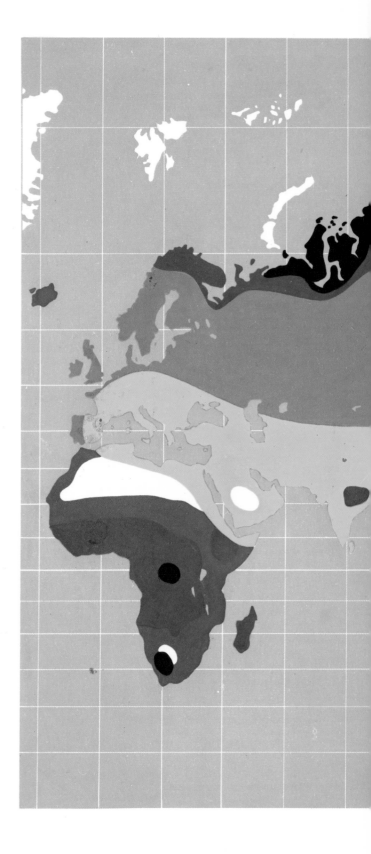

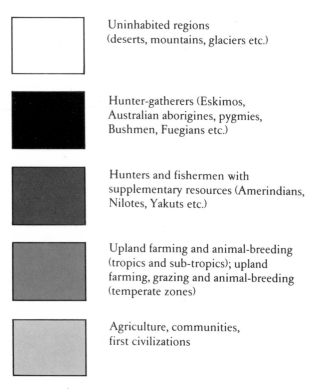

Uninhabited regions
(deserts, mountains, glaciers etc.)

Hunter-gatherers (Eskimos,
Australian aborigines, pygmies,
Bushmen, Fuegians etc.)

Hunters and fishermen with
supplementary resources (Amerindians,
Nilotes, Yakuts etc.)

Upland farming and animal-breeding
(tropics and sub-tropics); upland
farming, grazing and animal-breeding
(temperate zones)

Agriculture, communities,
first civilizations

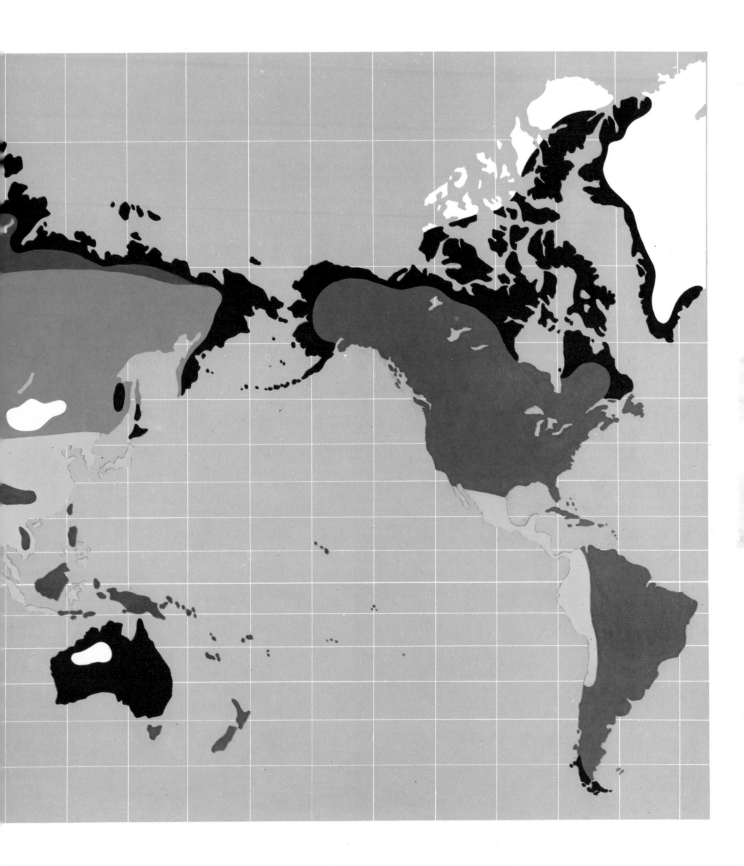

8   Man comes of age

In this final chapter we are concerned with the sweeping changes that brought mankind from primitive obscurity to the dawn of civilization. We no longer need to think in terms of the hundreds of thousands, even millions of years that it took ape-man to evolve into man, *Homo habilis* into *Homo erectus* into *Homo sapiens*. The story of man's journey from Upper Palaeolithic cave to Bronze and Iron Age city unfolds over a mere dozen millennia or so.

Cultural rather than physical evolution now determined human progress. Man's mind had developed to the point where he could adjust so quickly and effectively to changes in his surroundings that there was no need for new, more 'advanced' species of *Homo* to appear. The changes in climate and vegetation brought about by the retreat of the glaciers between 15,000 and 10,000 BC wrought havoc among much of the animal kingdom — in North America the mammoth and horse died out, in Europe and Asia the reindeer and horse retreated, the woolly mammoth and bison became extinct. *Homo sapiens sapiens,* who had relied upon such animals for survival, neither retreated nor became extinct, but used his intelligence to search for food elsewhere. In certain parts of the world he sought for the first time to control nature by selecting and breeding particular plants and animals for his own use, and thereby invented agriculture.

As people multiplied on the basis of the new economy, colonizing previously uninhabited regions and expanding within known ones, human ingenuity was taxed to the limit. How could farming which had been suitable for the relatively dry, thinly forested Mediterranean lands be adapted to new territories such as wet, thickly forested northern and central Europe? Man thought of the answer with greater use

Homo sapiens sapiens: *a woman of the Bronze Age.*

of damp-resistant wheat and sturdy cattle. How could a valley in southern Iran which had supported three villages be made to support six? Man invented irrigation and doubled his annual crop yield.

To begin with these advances came only slowly, though at a breakneck speed by Palaeolithic standards. Primitive farming, associated with the New Stone Age or 'Neolithic', took four thousand years to reach Britain from its original home in the Near East. Irrigation only became widespread in Iran three thousand years after the first introduction of farming there. Yet as the population continued to expand so the great wheel of change gathered momentum.

In order to cope with the increasing complexity of life, societies transformed themselves from loose-knit bands and tribes into tightly organized chiefdoms and states. Much greater emphasis was now placed on status and rank, and elaborate chains of command ensured that decisions taken by chiefs and priest-kings at the centre were put into effect by the lower orders at the fringes. Craftsmen grew in number and specialized more and more in their different trades. Potters, weavers and flint-knappers were joined by the first metalsmiths, wheelwrights and shipbuilders as the Neolithic gave way to the Bronze Age. Little more than two thousand years later, less in some places, the succeeding Iron Age had introduced yet another metal industry, and yet more changes. Today the wheel is spinning so fast we expect to experience change on an almost daily basis. Many have witnessed the development of the motor car, powered flight, the atomic bomb and computers all in one lifetime. It is a far cry from the 500,000-year gap between the discovery of fire and the invention of farming.

But of course these great economic and technological breakthroughs did not occur simultaneously across the globe. One has only to look around the world today to realize that different societies are at very different stages of development. This was not the case in Palaeolithic times. Although some regions were more progressive than others, all people throughout the then inhabited parts of the world depended for their livelihood upon hunting and the gathering of wild foods. With the introduction of farming this pattern of uniformity disappeared for ever. Some environments were better suited to the new economy than others, and while farming villages sprang up in these areas, later to be followed by towns, cities and civilization, the rest of the world remained essentially unchanged, still leading a largely Palaeolithic way of life. Today we have the Stone Age and the Computer Age side by side.

The end of the Ice Age

Now we must retrace our steps to take a closer look at the twilight era of Palaeolithic man.

Some 17,000 years ago (15,000 BC) the glaciers had reached their maximum extent. In the great park tundra belt bordering the ice-sheets, from northern Germany to northern Spain and from eastern Europe to the Atlantic, Upper Palaeolithic man had established a flourishing way of life, based mainly on the hunting of abundant reindeer, horse, bison and woolly mammoth. Magdalenian folk in the west and late Gravettian folk in the east (both named after sites in southern France) moved seasonally in small bands across the open landscape following their prey. Where they could they found shelter in caves and hollows, as for instance in southern France and northern Spain, whose famous cave art bears witness to the richness of life at the time. Late Gravettian hunters in eastern Europe and Russia, by and large less well endowed with natural rock shelters, were capable of building snug tent-like huts, partially dug into the ground and roofed with tough hides on frameworks of giant mammoth bones. Several of these huts might be grouped together to form quite a large encampment, perhaps the seasonal base of half a dozen families or more.

The pattern of life was much the same in the New World. Restricted by the ice-sheets to the plains south of a line running roughly from modern Seattle through St Louis to New York, North American bands migrated seasonally in pursuit of large herds of

Mammoth ribs, covered over with skins, made huts in regions such as eastern Europe where cave shelters were not easily found.

mammoths, bison, camels and horses. Like their Old World counterparts, these hunters chose natural caves for shelter, but could if necessary build primitive huts in the open.

The big-game hunting way of life lasted for several thousand years, in Europe for five thousand years or more. But by 10,000 BC it was doomed. All around the hunters the landscape was changing. The Pleistocene epoch was giving way to the Holocene ('Recent Times'). Slowly but surely the ice caps were retreating

to their focal points in Scandinavia, the Alps and western and eastern Canada. As the glaciers melted the seas rose, drowning great coastal grazing grounds in western Europe. Still 100 metres below the level of the present day around 15,000 BC, by 11,000 BC the seas had risen to less than 50 m below, and by 7500 BC only 25 m below. The land-bridge linking North America with Asia was submerged to become the Bering Strait by 8000 BC; by 6000 BC the English Channel was flooded and Britain cut off from Europe.

The climate and vegetation underwent an equally marked transformation. In northern Europe, where most research has been done, we know that the open tundra gave way during the ninth millennium BC to

forests of birch and pine. These were themselves superseded over the next two thousand years by much denser and damper forests of oak mixed with hazel, elm, alder and lime.

From the Palaeolithic hunter's point of view perhaps the most catastrophic change, however, was the decline and eventual disappearance of the vast herds of big game. The encroaching forests and swelling seas drastically reduced the open plains available for grazing. As we have seen, in Europe the reindeer and horse retreated north with the tundra, and the bison and woolly mammoth died out; in North America, of the principal big game hunted by Late Palaeolithic man, only the bison survived (it was

185

left to hunters of the 19th century AD, almost to finish off the bison). Luckily for European man, the advance of medium-sized game with the forests helped to partially fill the gap left by the large herbivores. Red deer, roe deer, elk, aurochs (ancestral cattle) and wild pig all spread northwards as the climate improved, although in far fewer numbers than the animals they replaced. Antelope and gazelle, as well as wild sheep and goats, increased rapidly in the southern and eastern Mediterranean lands. New World hunters were not so fortunate. Although the bison remained in large numbers in northern regions, elsewhere only a few medium-sized game animals survived to provide a limited supply of meat, although small rodents like rabbits and squirrels abounded and supplemented the diet.

How did prehistoric man cope with this transformation of his surroundings? Throughout the northern hemisphere generally there was an undoubted shift towards greater consumption of plant foods and smaller game animals: the warming up of the climate and the expansion of the forests made this almost inevitable if man were to survive. But at a regional level the pattern is much less uniform. If we concentrate on the European evidence for a moment, and divide up this long epoch of change into three chronological bands—before 10,000 BC, 10,000 to 8000 BC, and after 8000 BC—we find a fascinating mosaic of human adaptations.

We have seen how in northern and western Europe before 10,000 BC the Magdalenian and late Gravettian hunters pursued large herbivores across an open tundra landscape. Their contemporaries around the shores of the Mediterranean were much more thinly scattered, relying upon those medium-sized game animals, such as the red and roe deer, that were the natural fauna of the temperate and boreal forests. There is some evidence that the bow and arrow were invented at this time around the North African coast; they would have been a more effective weapon against the flighty deer than the powerful but cumbersome spear of the northern hunters. Minute worked flints known as 'microliths' came into fashion at much the same period, used principally to tip arrows without overweighting them.

Between 10,000 and 8000 BC this Mediterranean adaptation spread north with the advancing birch and pine forests. In France the Magdalenian reindeer

hunters were supplanted by poorer groups, known as 'Azilians' after the French cave site of Mas d'Azil, who introduced the bow and arrow and microliths to Europe in their quest for deer. Whether the Azilians were in fact new immigrants arriving from the south, or whether they were former big-game hunters who had learnt the new way of life from their southern neighbours we do not know. We do know, however, that they were much thinner on the ground than their predecessors, so it seems likely that many of the Palaeolithic hunters either died out or migrated north with the reindeer. For a short time they enjoyed something of a renaissance in northern Germany, where the retreating ice opened up new grazing grounds; encampments which have been found show how these hunters could rely much more heavily on one abundant species, the reindeer, than their counterparts farther south. But it was not long before the sea came flooding in, drowning the newly exposed land and creating the Baltic Sea.

In the meantime, around the eastern shores of the Mediterranean even more momentous changes were taking place. While contemporaries along the North African coast concentrated on deer and such antelope as the gnu and hartebeest, people in the Levant were in the process of making that historic shift from hunting and gathering to the nurturing of natural foods. They were fortunate to live in a region where stands of wild wheat and barley grew thickly in the uplands. Already by 13,000 BC primitive grinders had begun to be used to process these cereals. Now, between 10,000 and 8000 BC a whole new way of life sprang up based on the systematic gathering of these wild plants. It is known as the 'Natufian', after the site of Wadi en-Natuf in Palestine where it was first recognized. The Natufians had a great inventory of reaping knives (sickles), querns, pestles and mortars to harvest and process the grain. The stability of their food supply enabled them to build the first villages, and encouraged them also to build 'villages' in the after-life for their dead—the first cemeteries. Eynan (Ain Mallaha) in Palestine is the best-known Natufian site. Here the settlement consisted of about fifty round huts, each 8 m in diameter and dug 1 m into the ground; the rubble walls were coated with plaster.

Mesolithic hunter with spear, bow and arrows and a knife.

The badly worn teeth of the inhabitants show that they had a coarse, gritty diet mainly of poorly processed plant foods, especially cereals. But the large number of gazelle bones demonstrates the important place of this animal in the economy as well. Recent research has even suggested that the gazelle may have been herded rather than hunted, yet another possible indication of the shift towards farming and animal husbandry.

The Natufians, for all their advanced characteristics, were still very much linked with their Palaeolithic forebears. The farming economy of the future—cultivated wheat and barley combined with domesticated sheep, goats, pigs and cattle—was only dimly discernible in their way of life. They neither made pottery nor wove textiles, but carried on the old bone-carving tradition of their ancestors. It was left to their successors to effect the so-called 'food-producing revolution' after 8000 BC and to usher in the Neolithic era.

Before we turn to this momentous development in human history we must refocus our attention on northern Europe, where we left the Azilians and dwindling Magdalenians in the tenth and ninth millennia BC. Before the sequence of events in the Near East was known about, archaeologists working in Europe defined what they termed a Middle Stone Age, or 'Mesolithic' era, which they imagined each Palaeolithic society went through before reaching the

Neolithic era and an agricultural way of life. The Mesolithic as defined for Europe never really took place in the Near East, mainly because the climatic transformation from Pleistocene to Holocene was not nearly so noticeable here. But what did the Mesolithic in Europe consist of?

The true Mesolithic belongs to the third of our chronological bands spanning the end of the Ice Age, taking us from 8000 BC to the arrival of farming in Europe some 3000 or 4000 years later. It is largely contemporary with the birth and growth of the first agriculture in the Near East (the first true Neolithic). By now the Azilians in France had given way to the Sauveterrians (also named after a French site), the Magdalenians in northern Germany and elsewhere to the earliest Maglemosians (from the Danish *magle mose* meaning 'great bog', a name appropriate for the conditions of the time). These labels have scant meaning in human terms, for there is little to choose between the microliths of the two groups. What differences there are reflect the varying opportunities for survival and expansion provided by the environment. On this criterion the Sauveterrians were a good deal worse off. They, and their successors after 6000 BC the Tardenoisians, suffered much denser forest growth than their northern neighbours. They were reduced by any standards to an impoverished existence, catching deer, fowl or small rodents where they could, turning no doubt to nuts, roots and edible fungi to augment their diet. Gone long ago was the cave art of their ancestors; such bonework as they produced has been leached away by the acidity of the sandy soils.

By contrast the Maglemosian folk developed a way of life that in its ingenuity and complexity bears comparison with the Eskimo adaptation to the Arctic

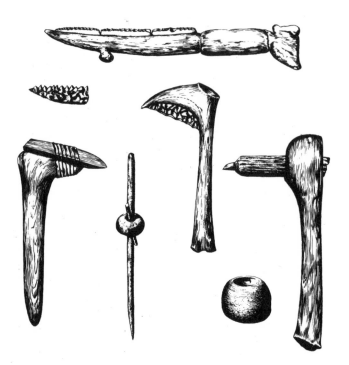

Tools of the late Stone Age. They include a Natufian carved bone reaping knife from Mount Carmel, Palestine (top) *and an adze and a pick set in wooden handles.*

A Neolithic farmer of the 5th millennium BC sharpening a stone axe. ▷

Overleaf: *A typical farming settlement of the Neolithic. The huts are rectangular and spacious; corn is cut with sickles and the grain is ground on stone slabs; livestock is domesticated and the art of making clay vessels well established. Man is achieving more and more control over his environment.*

Mesolithic hunter-fishers of South America fishing with bows and arrows. Much of this simple way of life still survives in the remoter parts.

several thousand years later. The picture we need to hold in our minds is of a Britain still joined to Europe (till 6000 BC) and of a great wealth of natural resources—medium-sized game, wild fowl, shellfish, fish—in and around the Rhine and Thames, which then meandered several hundred miles further than they do today towards the north, combining to form a giant, fertile estuary in what is now the North Sea. At its peak the Maglemosian way of life extended from Britain right across to western Russia; but the focus of settlement was probably around this colossal estuary. Many sites have been found along the coasts of eastern Britain and Denmark; many more must lie buried at the bottom of the North Sea. It is no coincidence that a Maglemosian harpoon was dredged up from between the Leman and Ower Banks, 25 miles off the Norfolk coast.

One of the earliest and best-known of such sites is Star Carr on the Yorkshire coast. Here many of the characteristics of the classic Mesolithic can be seen: an extensive use of bone and antler, particularly for harpoons and simple picks; large, flat axes and adzes for felling trees; and a reliance on a wide range of foods, animal and vegetable, though red deer predominated. Evidence among the animal bones suggests that man had, for the first time in the Old World, domesticated the dog, while wooden paddles show that he had already learnt to build primitive watercraft, probably dugout canoes to judge by finds made elsewhere in Scotland and Holland. Most intriguing of all, however, was the discovery of twenty-one masks made from the front portions of stag skulls, with the antlers left in place; these could have had some magical or ritual function, or alternatively they might have been worn as disguises by the hunters during the chase. Four or five family groups occupied Star Carr every winter for about twenty years around 7500 BC, living in shelters on a platform of branches and brushwood next to a lake. No doubt they followed the deer inland during the summer months.

This seasonal movement from lake shore and coast in winter to upland in summer was a pattern that became intensified as the Mesolithic wore on. The creation of the North and Baltic Seas in the seventh and sixth millennia BC meant not only that great tracts of land were no longer available for the grazing deer and other animals that man depended on, but also

that the areas of coast were now much more extensive, both in absolute terms and in relation to the total land mass. It was only natural therefore for late Mesolithic folk to begin to exploit coastal resources in earnest. The simple dugout canoes of the eighth millennium must have developed into sea-going vessels, for we find bones of deep-sea fish as well as seals, porpoises, sea birds and land mammals at coastal sites of the time. Even more strikingly, great mounds of discarded shells called 'kitchen middens' now begin to appear all round the coasts of Denmark and elsewhere, representing man's first attempt to exploit the highly productive beds of oysters, cockles and mussels that were available in shallow water.

It has never been proved that shellfish were the main source of food for the shore-dwellers—scientific analysis of a Mesolithic shell site at Morton, eastern Scotland, for instance, has shown that although there was a much greater volume of shells than of animal and fish bones, the shells represented much less in terms of meat weight. Even so the appearance of the middens is significant. In terms of natural availability shellfish are more productive per acre than any other form of meat, but they require the expenditure of a great deal of time and energy in collection and preparation—much more than for other hunting and gathering pursuits. The introduction of shell-gathering suggests, therefore, that human societies were now more closely knit and better organized to carry out collective activities than they had been in Palaeolithic times. As we shall see, a study of the contemporary development of farming in the Near East leads to much the same conclusion.

But what of the rest of the world at this time? Our brief look at events in northern Europe has in fact provided us with a useful key to developments elsewhere, for the retreating ice and rising seas afflicted the inhabitants of North and South America, south-east Asia and Australia as much as it did their Old World counterparts, and the solutions chosen were much the same everywhere.

In North America around 7000 BC we enter the era known as the 'Archaic', to be equated with the European Mesolithic. Archaic folk relied upon a much broader range of animals and plants than their big-game hunting predecessors. They made coiled baskets, millstones, mortars and pestles for collecting and grinding seeds and nuts, and small

In southern Asia and the islands of Melanesia, the rising seas after the retreat of the ice encouraged the hunters to take to the water. From crude beginnings such as these came larger, sea-going boats, capable of reaching Australia.

The suspension bridge made of twisted lianas is a device with a very long history in South America.

projectile heads for spearing the few deer, antelope and other small game. Like the Maglemosians they learnt how to fish — the fish-hooks found at many sites prove this — and ate quantities of shellfish on the coasts. Their way of life was well suited to their surroundings, and survived in barren regions like the Desert West until the nineteenth century AD — in eastern parts agriculture had been introduced from Mexico long before the birth of Christ.

Less is known about life in South America at this time, but here too people seem to have depended upon a wider variety of foods after 7000 BC, with a seasonal exploitation of the different resources in upland and lowland environments. One animal which is unique to South America, the llama of the camel family, was eventually tamed and domesticated (perhaps as early as the sixth millennium BC) to act as a beast of burden between the mountains and the lowlands, although it was also exploited to a lesser extent for its meat and wool. Much of this simple hunting and gathering way of life was superseded

along the coasts of Chile and Peru by a more settled existence after 5000 BC, later to be followed by the first South American civilizations. But in some parts of tropical Latin America, east of the Andes, the primitive hunter-fishers survive to this day, to remind us how our Mesolithic ancestors might have lived.

The rising seas of the postglacial period also forced people in south-east Asia and Australia to congregate more in coastal areas in search of food. Huge middens of seashells provide a striking parallel with the late Maglemosian middens of northern Europe, and appear at much the same time and for much the same reasons in both parts of the world. In addition to shellfish the south-east Asians ate sharks, sting rays and fish which they caught from primitive boats, invented presumably even earlier to effect the colonization of Australia. Near the coast they hunted pigs, deer, wild oxen, rhinoceroses, elephants and monkeys, together with small rodents, and gathered almonds, betel nuts, beans and gourds. Many of these local plants began to be cultivated before very long, as

man took the first tentative steps towards the control of nature. In the Near East the 'food-producing revolution' had occurred several millennia earlier.

The first farmers

We have already seen how hunters and gatherers in the Levant, known as Natufians, had started to harvest wild wheat and barley between 10,000 and 8000 BC, and had built the first villages and cemeteries. Contemporaries on the upper Euphrates and the south Iranian plateau had also begun to collect plants more intensively, particularly the wild cereals. Now, in all three of these areas as well as Anatolia during the eighth and seventh millennia BC, man passed across the revolutionary threshold between merely gathering wild foods and actually trying to control and nurture them. He planted cereals and pulses, and discovered that while some animals, such as gazelle, had to be kept away from the fields as uncontrollable crop pests, others, such as sheep and goat, could be tamed and herded, thus providing a ready supply of meat, milk and wool and an alternative source of food if the harvest failed.

Other animals were 'domesticated' in this way, as man slowly learnt the best combinations of the resources at his disposal during this new Neolithic epoch. Late in the seventh millennium cattle began to be herded on the great upland plateau of central Anatolia, where it was found that sheep and cattle could be supported on the same piece of land because sheep (and goats) could feed on shorter grasses than cattle. Pigs had already been tamed in smaller numbers in the mountains of eastern Turkey and Iran; their tremendous fecundity, ten times that of cows or ewes, their rapid growth and their ability to eat almost anything would quickly have become apparent to the early farmers.

The physical characteristics of these plants and animals changed subtly as domestication proceeded.

Man took a decisive step forward when he discovered that some animals could be tamed and used—either as haulers of loads (left) or, like the llama and guanaco of South America (opposite), as beasts of burden and providers of meat, milk and wool. This step was taken at widely differing periods—in the Near East, for example, about ten thousand years ago, but much later in the New World.

The ears of wild wheat and barley had split on ripening in order to scatter the grain; man on the other hand found it easier to collect ears with a genetic mutation preventing the grain from being dispersed, and thus consciously or unconsciously selected more seed corn with the deviant mutation than without; gradually cereals with ears which did not split came to predominate in the fields. In a similar way the early herders tended to select smaller, more docile cattle and sheep; the herds were now protected from their natural predators in the wild (by dogs, also newly domesticated, as well as men), and so the smaller breeds prevailed, which led to a reduction in horn size as well.

This first primitive agriculture was the base upon which all subsequent advances were founded. Even at this early stage farming was so productive that it could support ten times as many people in a given area of land as the foraging way of life of the late Palaeolithic. Villages, which had been rare among the Natufians, now sprang up everywhere on the upland plateaux, with houses that were built to last, equipped with fixed corn-grinders, ovens and storage space for grain. The easily built round huts of the Natufians gave way to rectangular dwellings which were easier to add on to, and reflect more permanent settlement.

Profound social changes came about with the more settled way of life. Palaeolithic hunter-gatherers had never claimed ownership of land or developed a real sense of territoriality because of their mobile existence and the variety of plants and animals in different environments that they could live on. Neolithic farmers on the other hand depended upon a much narrower range of foods, in particular their crops, which they could only grow on certain soils in certain places. Thus good land became an important possession, to be tended and guarded by the whole village, and passed on intact to succeeding generations. Elaborate rules of marriage and descent were introduced to ensure continuity of land ownership and to establish the stronger social ties needed to bind the community together for defence.

◁ *The earliest pots were built up by hand from clay coils, and were probably made by women, judging from research among modern primitive tribes.*

In the 4th millennium BC a simple 'wheel' was introduced for throwing pots, which speeded up the production and helped give the wares of one workshop greater uniformity.

The new rules of inheritance did not apply only to land. People who had previously been able to carry around little or nothing as mobile hunter-gatherers now found that they could accumulate personal possessions in their houses and wear expensive finery. The demand for rare and precious goods stimulated the development of the first real trade. Obsidian, a shiny black volcanic glass originating in central Anatolia and round Lake Van, travelled enormous distances, probably through the medium of ceremonial gift exchange between villages. Some of the obsidian from Van was exchanged so many times that eventually it reached villages 560 miles away in the Zagros Mountains in southern Iran. Flints, turquoise and other semi-precious stones were also much sought after.

New crafts came into being with the new way of life. It was found that one of the best ways to make cereals digestible was to boil them, but some suitable receptacle was needed. Fired pottery bowls proved to be the answer, and the earliest examples known date from about 7000 BC in the Zagros region. At this early date they were made by building up coils of clay in rings which were then squeezed into shape by hand.

◁ *Fired pottery is known from as early as 7000 BC—fired, presumably, in open-air kilns built up of turf sods and demolished after one firing.*

Weaving on a primitive loom. Division of labour between the sexes was an inevitable trend as community life began to grow more complex.

The technique probably derived from the coiled baskets that were also in use at the time. Research among modern primitive tribes suggests that the Neolithic coiled pots would have been made by women, a reflection of another important social trend, the increasing division of labour into jobs done by men and jobs done by women. This would of course have existed to a limited extent in the Palaeolithic era—few women would have been strong enough to knap flints for any length of time, for instance. But the growing range of jobs to be done in the Neolithic economy forced a rapid acceleration of the process. Spinning and weaving (mainly of wool), another important invention of the seventh millennium, would have been done by women too. The farmer's home was, in fact, very much a place of work, where his wife and daughters ground grain, coiled pots and baskets, cooked, and wove garments against the winter cold.

The importance of the home and the continuity of life from generation to generation found expression in the new cult of ancestor worship. At Jericho in Palestine the dead were buried under the houses, but decapitated, the skulls being filled with tinted plaster, and given cowrie and other shells for eyes to look like living faces, and kept above ground to be venerated. Man's first attempts to control nature also called for other kinds of ritual. There was no division of life into separate religious and practical aspects as there is today—then it was just as important to propitiate the spirits at the first sowing of the seed corn as it was to choose the right soil and the right time of year. The great cult of the mother goddess which spread with the farmers therefore reflected man's new concern for fertility—the fertility of his soil, his crops, his livestock and his womenfolk (children had been a burden to Palaeolithic hunters on the move, but were now essential not merely as heirs but also as labourers in the fields or highly prized 'possessions' to be exchanged in marriage for goods or land).

At one famous farming site, Çatal Hüyük in south-central Anatolia, all the different aspects of the new way of life are combined together to give us an idea of what Neolithic man could achieve. By the late seventh millennium BC Çatal Hüyük had grown to be one of the first small towns in the world, a flourishing community of about six thousand souls living in perhaps a thousand closely packed houses, extending over 32 acres. The houses were of mud brick, built back to back so that entry was possible only via the roof (which was flat); the edge of the town would therefore have presented a forbidding blank façade to any potential aggressor.

The prosperity of the town was based on agriculture and trade. Three different kinds of wheat (emmer, einkorn and bread wheat), barley, peas and vetches grew in the fields, while herds of cattle and sheep grazed near by. The diet was supplemented to some extent by the gathering of pistachios, almonds, crab apples, juniper and hackberry, probably also root vegetables and soft fruits. Red deer and wild birds were hunted too. The town is even more significant as a centre of trade. The inhabitants may have held a monopoly in the supply of obsidian, which they quarried in the nearby volcanic mountains and worked into beautiful knives and unique circular mirrors. Other skilled craftsmen turned Syrian flints into daggers, Mediterranean seashells into ornaments, and tiny nuggets of native (pure, unsmelted) copper into beads; many of these products were then traded far and wide. In addition the womenfolk wove textiles and made baskets and pots for local use.

The most remarkable feature of the Çatal Hüyük community, however, was its artistic and religious life. In among the small mud huts were numerous shrines, built on the normal rectangular plan, but decorated inside with an extraordinary variety of painted frescoes, carved stone figurines, recessed outlines of animals and modelled bulls' heads with actual horn cores incorporated. The unifying theme was fertility and the cult of the great mother goddess, who was depicted variously giving birth to bulls, rams and children. Opposed to this creative force was the death cult, represented by giant vultures swooping down on headless human beings. Here we have epitomized the main concerns of Neolithic man, his awareness of the unity of life and death and his need to come to terms with both. They are concerns which, in the shape of the supreme goddess, were to reach their climax in the Bronze Age civilizations.

For grinding corn, Neolithic women used two stones, one hand-size and one large, flat and smooth—distant ancestors of the pestle and mortar.

The spread of farming

We have noted that one important characteristic of farming was its ability to support and encourage the growth of population. Towns like Çatal Hüyük were one of the results, but even the fertile plateau of central Anatolia could not continue to absorb growing numbers of people when agriculture was at such a primitive level. One solution was to increase the quantities of cereals produced each year by improving the techniques of farming: irrigation and the plough were two such innovations which gradually superseded the old methods over the next few thousand years. But there was an easier alternative which involved less effort: emigration and the colonization of new land.

Already by 6000 BC farmers had settled on light, easily farmed soils near the edges of rivers and drying lakes in Greece and Macedonia. They introduced the first wheat, barley and lentils, domestic sheep, cattle and pigs to mainland Europe and made the first permanent settlements and pottery here. It was the initial stage in a great expansion of agriculture that was to reach up through the Balkans to central Europe by 4700 BC, across to northern France and the Netherlands by 4000 BC, and eventually to Britain and the rest of northern Europe between 3500 and 3000 BC.

To what extent this involved an actual movement of peoples, as opposed to indigenous Mesolithic folk simply adopting a new way of life, it is hard to say. Prehistorians are more wary today than their predecessors used to be of saying that change in the material base of society necessarily implies a change in population. But when we consider that Neolithic societies would have grown much more rapidly than their Mesolithic counterparts, and that few of the farming settlements in Europe were situated in landscapes favoured by earlier hunter-fishers, it seems a fair assumption that farming spread initially by the migration of peoples rather than of ideas alone.

This conjecture is supported by evidence from the Mediterranean, where Neolithic colonists travelled not overland, through thickly forested valleys and plains, but by sea — until modern times much the quickest if most hazardous mode of transport. Mediterranean islands over 30 miles distant from the mainland, such as Crete and Cyprus, had never been colonized in the Palaeolithic era because the distances had been too great for the primitive watercraft of the time. But Neolithic man developed a highly efficient polished-stone axe which enabled him to fell and hollow out trees large enough to carry him, his family and kin, together with their livestock and seed corn, across the critical 30 miles of water separating overcrowded mainland from fertile, virgin island. By 6000 BC we find simple farming communities, with the usual array of crops and domestic animals, firmly established in Crete and Cyprus, where previously there had been no human occupation whatsoever — proof enough of the movement of people, not just ideas.

Sea transport meant that farming spread much quicker in the Mediterranean than in the Balkans and northern Europe. The island of Corsica, like Crete and Cyprus uninhabited in the Palaeolithic, has recently produced a startling series of radiocarbon dates suggesting that it was first settled by farmers without pottery in the late 7th millennium BC. Even if we discount these early dates as an error, we are still left with a significant body of evidence indicating that Corsica, Sicily, Sardinia, Mallorca, and the coastal regions of southern Italy, southern France and eastern Spain had all adopted pottery and, to a greater or lesser extent, agriculture by the end of the 6th millennium BC. The contrast between the speed at

Clay-lined grain storage pit. Making provision for the future by storing some of the produce was an important advance, symbolized in Chapter 41 of the Book of Genesis.

The plough — the biggest single advance in the technology of farming. Its introduction greatly improved the productivity of the land, and enabled man to colonize even the poorest soils.

which farming spread overland through Europe and by sea through the Mediterranean is brought into sharpest relief if we look at France. Here the Neolithic had taken firm root in the south by 5000 BC, colonized by sea, whereas the earliest agriculture in the north, introduced from central Europe and ultimately the Balkans, did not become established until over 1000 years later.

In pointing up this contrast, however, we are not really comparing like with like. The Mediterranean Neolithic was in many ways very different from that in temperate Europe to the north. A large number of the earliest coastal sites in the Mediterranean called 'Neolithic' were in fact merely 'Mesolithic' sites which had adopted pottery—that is to say, the indigenous hunting-and-fishing way of life carried on, but with the addition of pot-making as a craft. A fully Neolithic economy, which included the sowing of crops and herding of animals, was usually only possible away from the coasts, on the strictly limited

areas of light river-deposited soil suitable for the primitive farming of the time. Thus in the Mediterranean we find a curious difference between coastal and inland sites. Caves and shell middens near the seashore, which had been occupied for thousands of years by Mesolithic folk, probably continued to be used for hunting by descendants of the same people, now making pottery, well into the Neolithic. Why should they change their ways when plentiful deer roamed inland and abundant tunny fish, some the

◁ *House-building in prehistoric Europe: pitched roofs and wattle-and-daub walls were necessary to withstand a rainy climate.*

In the Danubian Neolithic, decoration, on pottery and textiles as well as on walls, suggest that thought was beginning to be exercised beyond the bare necessities of existence.

weight of adult cattle, shoaled seasonally in front of their cave mouths, needing only to be caught from boats?

By contrast immigrants from the east, trained in the laborious but productive arts of cereal farming and animal husbandry, sought light, fertile soils inland. In particular they settled the eastern part of Sicily in the vicinity of modern Catania, the Adriatic coast of Dalmatia near present-day Split, and the richest land on the east coast of Italy: the Tavoliere,

south and west of the Gargano Peninsula. To give an example of the speed with which the new settlers colonized these environments, and of the favourable conditions they found, one need only consider the Tavoliere. Here, within the space of a millennium or so, over 300 settlements had sprung up in a previously uninhabited landscape of some 240 sq. km. Each settlement consisted of a ditched enclosure, covering about 20 hectares (40 ha at one site) and used presumably as a kind of large animal pen for the domestic sheep, goats, cattle and pigs. The huts within the enclosures seem to have been built on stilts, perhaps as a precaution against the periodic floods that watered the crops, which were principally bread wheat, followed by barley and various pulses. Each community comprised 50 souls or more, who would have spent their time much as did their contemporaries in the Near East, tending their crops and animals, grinding corn, weaving textiles, making and painting pots and even working obsidian, which was traded from the volcanic island of Lipari, some 220 miles away to the south-west.

By and large there were fewer native Mesolithic hunters and gatherers in the Balkans than in the Mediterranean, and so the Neolithic colonists settling the valleys and plains of Bulgaria, Romania, Yugoslavia and Hungary in the 6th millennium BC found little local competition. Their problem was to adapt the way of life their ancestors had pioneered in the Near East to the colder, wetter and more thickly forested climes of south-eastern Europe. Houses could no longer be flat-roofed and made of mud-brick: pitched roofs and *pisé* (rammed earth) or, to the north, wattle-and-daub construction were developed to withstand the heavy rains. Until the forests could be cleared substantially to provide grazing grounds, wild game probably made up as high a proportion of the meat diet as the domestic sheep, cattle and pig. But these first Balkan farmers were still recognizably the offspring of their Asian forefathers. They planted wheat and barley, albeit more damp-resistant strains, and shaped and painted pots and goddess figurines, even if of a unique variety. Many of their villages were substantial and permanent enough to form large mounds, as in the Near East. Clay stamps with check patterns were used to decorate the first textiles in the area, while ornaments made from the shells of *Spondylus,* the thorny oyster of the Aegean, were traded the full length of the Balkans, demonstrating that the desire for self-adornment was as strong here as it was in Anatolia or the Levant.

In the 5th millennium BC Balkan colonists settled the great belt of arable loess (wind-blown sand) which stretches 1000 miles from Hungary to Holland along the Danube and the Rhine. The way of life they pioneered, known as the Danubian, was one stage still further removed from its oriental ancestry. Rainfall was even heavier here, forest growth even thicker. Sharper axes were used to fell the towering oak trees and convert them into logs and posts for their characteristic wooden houses, usually 16 m long, often over 30 m. Social customs must have been markedly different from those farther south, for these buildings would have housed several families under one roof, together with some of their livestock and grain. Eight of the 'long houses' might be grouped together to form a village, and the inhabitants would have shared a communal 'club house', anything up to 100 m long, where stories might be told and rituals chanted to while away winter evenings and ward off evil spirits lurking in the forests.

Many Danubian settlements had palisaded enclosures attached, used it is thought for herds of cattle. In the colder, wetter conditions of temperate Europe cattle had superseded sheep and goat as the principal domestic animals, perhaps the most fundamental shift away from the pattern of the Balkan Neolithic. Even so, contact with the south was maintained, as is proved by the extraordinary perseverance of the trade in *Spondylus* shell ornaments, which reached from the Aegean right to the source of the Danube. Exchange of other goods over shorter distances helped keep Danubian folk in regular touch with one another. At the famous site of Köln-Lindenthal in West Germany, for instance, stone axes were excavated which had come from 70 miles away, while the source of the clay for the distinctive Danubian 'linear-stroked' pottery lay some 50 miles off. From such small beginnings developed the complex trades in flints, salt, amber and ultimately copper and tin which were to be such a feature of Late Neolithic and Bronze Age Europe.

To begin with, however, the effect of trade and growth of population was to bring the farming peoples of central Europe into contact for the first time with those Mesolithic folk who had established,

Domestication of the horse may have taken place in palisaded enclosures, by methods not so different from those in use today.

Overleaf: *The raising of livestock —cattle, sheep, goats and pigs—was well established by the Late Neolithic in Europe.*

as we saw earlier, such a successful way of life along the coasts of north-western Europe. Initially the result was much as it had been when farmers first explored the Mediterranean. The native hunter-fishers adopted pottery, but otherwise continued in the ways of their ancestors; the new settlers meanwhile colonized the lightest, most fertile soils inland. Nevertheless gradually there was an intermingling of life styles, with groups sharing elements of both Neolithic and Mesolithic parentage. Unlike their Danubian forebears, for instance, these people of the coasts were accomplished seafarers, a skill inherited from late Mesolithic folk. In the 4th and 3rd millennia BC they made the western seaways their own, settling lowland Britain and Ireland and erecting strange stone monuments to their dead all along the Atlantic seaboard, from Spain to Scandinavia.

These 'megaliths' as they are called (from the Greek for 'large stones') are among the most remarkable prehistoric structures ever built. Although they range from small stone rows to massive, awe-inspiring passage graves, used as communal tombs, they must surely represent some continuity of worship between these distant lands. Symbolic spirals and serpents carved on the stones link the monuments of Brittany and Ireland, corbelled roofs the chamber tombs of Newgrange on the River Boyne in Ireland and Maes Howe in Orkney. What is more, on radiocarbon evidence the megaliths are the earliest monumental stone structures in the world, or are at least partly contemporary with the oldest Mesopotamian temples of the 4th millennium BC.

The dawn of civilization

The expansion of farming on to the most easily cultivable soils from the Balkans to Ireland by the 4th millennium BC brought the Europeans face to face with the problem that had already confronted their Near Eastern counterparts: how could the growth in population be maintained? One solution was for people to move into the less hospitable uplands. From the very beginning of their colonization of Europe the farmers had made limited use of mountain pastures in summer for their sheep and goats, but now this exploitation was intensified dramatically. The lakeland regions of Switzerland, for instance, previously the preserve of Mesolithic deer

hunters, were gradually colonized by farmers moving south from Germany up the Rhine Valley and east up the Rhône Valley from France. With their crops and livestock they settled along the marshy — but treeless — margins of the lakes, building ingenious gabled dwellings which they stabilized by sinking wooden piles into the bog beneath. The size of each community depended upon the amount of arable land available near by, but a wealthy settlement, such as at Niederwil in northern Switzerland, might consist of 10 substantial long houses extending over 2800 square metres and surrounded by a wooden palisade.

Another solution to the problem of rising population and shortage of land was a technological one, the adoption of ploughing or irrigation to improve crop yields. In the Near East irrigation had already been developed in some areas by the late 6th millennium BC. As we saw at the beginning of this chapter, one valley in southern Iran, for instance, succeeded in doubling its output of crops by the introduction of irrigation around 5500 BC; instead of three villages the valley could now support six.

The controlling and artificial redirecting of water proved to be the key to the exploitation of the vast resources of the lowland Mesopotamian plains. Here the soils were naturally very rich, but suffered from alternate periods of drying-out and flood; what was required was the erection and annual maintenance of an enormous network of canals to prevent drought, and giant earthworks to prevent the rivers overflowing their banks. The only possible way this could be achieved in the days before mechanization was by the hard labour of hundreds of thousands of men. This in itself required that there should be some centralized authority capable both of organizing this work and of coercing the men to undertake it. The result was that communities in Mesopotamia (also in Egypt) which had in Early Neolithic times been loose-knit and egalitarian became transformed during the course of the 5th and 4th millennia into tightly organized states. Chiefs and priest-kings now controlled vast armies of peasant-slaves, while artisans

A Bronze Age warrior chieftain. Armour and weapons such as these have been found in tombs dating from late in the 2nd millennium BC, when the working of copper-tin alloys was well understood.

appeared, practising new crafts needed to run the state — scribes to record bureaucratic transactions, wheelwrights and shipbuilders to make the new vehicles and vessels necessary for improved communications, metalsmiths to provide sharper tools for the carpenters and weapons for the armies to defend the state. The characteristic features of what we think of as 'civilization' were in fact coalescing at this time in Mesopotamia and Egypt. Here the first cities, organized religions, priests, kings and scribes in

Bronze statuette of a bull from Býčí Skála.

instance, the agricultural base upon which civilization had to be founded took far longer to develop than in the Old World. This was because no large animals were available for domestication (other than the llama, restricted principally to the mountains of South America) and because maize, ultimately the main staple together with beans and squash, took 3000 years from its time of first domestication around 4500 BC to evolve into a plant substantial and productive enough to support large populations. Consequently the oldest New World civilizations, which are found in Central America, belong to the 2nd millennium BC and later. Only then do we find the earliest characteristic ceremonial buildings, fine art, craft specialization and, later, towns and cities. Similarly the Indus civilization of the 3rd millennium BC and the Shang civilization of the 2nd millennium BC, although the oldest civilizations in eastern Asia, were still several thousand years behind the pioneering centres of the Near East.

An adequate discussion of these foci of early civilization would require another book (Glyn Daniel's *The First Civilizations,* London 1968, is a good introduction). For present purposes, therefore, let us concentrate our attention once more on Europe, in the hope that here we may detect a pattern in the evolution of civilization which may be broadly applicable elsewhere in the world.

Although irrigation and ploughing were both first invented in the Near East as technological solutions to the problems of overcrowding and shortage of land, irrigation was for the Orient by far the most important innovation, as we have seen. In Europe it was the other way round. Here there were no naturally fertile flood-plains on the scale of the Nile

the world bear witness to the fact that, for much of the Near East at any rate, civilization had already dawned by 3000 BC.

For Europe and the rest of the world the process was rather more long drawn out. In the Americas, for

215

Woman of the pre-Celtic Bronze Age—a time when personal ornaments had reached a high level of elaborate craftsmanship.

or the Tigris and Euphrates, waiting to be tamed and controlled. Rainfall was in any case high enough and regular enough in most parts to make irrigation unnecessary. A much greater problem was the shortage of light soils for cultivation, and the difficulty of breaking up the more abundant heavier soils so that the crops could take root. The introduction of the plough was the answer. Right across northern Europe, from Britain to Poland, we find evidence of early ploughing by the very beginning of the 3rd millennium BC. Wooden yokes from Switzerland and a pot from Poland with two yoked oxen show the means of traction; criss-cross plough marks preserved under burial mounds at

South Street in Britain or Sarnowo in Poland indicate the method by which the soil was broken up.

The social consequences of the introduction of ploughing bear comparison with those that attended the development of irrigation in the Near East, if on a much more limited scale. Ploughing was a considerably more laborious pursuit than the crude but simple slash-and-burn agriculture that had preceded it, where the farmer had merely cleared an area by burning, hoed, planted and harvested his crops, and then moved to another area. Moreover, there would now have been competition for regions with the best and most easily arable land. The combined effect was to stimulate the growth of more centrally organized societies, probably chiefdoms, capable of apportioning land, settling disputes between rival groups, organizing the tilling or defence of land and redistributing goods between the increasingly diverse parts of the community. Organization and control from the centre enabled craftsmen to specialize more and more in their various trades, and traders to carry the products over growing distances. It is no coincidence that at this time — the 3rd millennium BC — we find, for instance, a marked intensification in flint mining, from the 360 shafts sunk at Grimes Graves in Norfolk to the 1000 shafts at Krzemionki in Poland. Traders carried not only flints, but also amber from the Baltic, *Spondylus* shells from the Aegean and innumerable other precious goods, hundreds of miles across Europe. Perhaps, however, the product most significant for the future that they traded was copper.

The colonization of the uplands and mountains of Europe in the 4th millennium BC inevitably brought farmers into contact with this attractively coloured, easily worked mineral, which is distributed especially in the Carpathians and Alps, but also in southern Germany, Spain and Ireland. Archaeologists have found a number of simple beads, pins and other ornaments in graves of that time in the Carpathian basin. These would have been produced merely by cold hammering, and required no specialized knowledge of metallurgy. When, however, the natural outcrops of copper began to run out, the farmers had to begin using first oxide ores from the surface, which require smelting at 1100 °C to separate the slag from the metal, and then sulphide ores, which, though more abundant, have to be mined, pounded to separate the mineral from the rock, roasted over several days to remove the sulphides, and then smelted like the oxide ores.

The great advantage of having laboriously heated and melted the copper to purify it was that it could then be poured into stone moulds and cast to produce functional tools and weapons, not just trinkets. Copper axes, adzes, chisels and awls were made in their thousands, and had a great influence, particularly on carpentry. The new tools were much sharper than their flint or stone equivalents, which is why we notice a considerable improvement in the techniques of woodworking in the 4th and 3rd millennia BC: the refinement of joints for houses, shares for ploughs and above all the development of the earliest wheeled vehicles, two-wheeled carts and four-wheeled wagons, evidence for which comes both from the Balkans and the Netherlands at this time.

The problem with these early copper tools and weapons was that they were much too soft to be durable — in fact as 'weapons' they were probably used more in ceremonies than in warfare, as we shall see. It was not until the very end of the 3rd millennium BC that metalsmiths discovered that by adding an alloy, at first antimony and arsenic, subsequently tin, they could vastly improve the strength of the metal. Today scientists employ what is known as the 'Vickers scale' to measure metal strength; using this scale we learn that copper in the unalloyed state has a hardness of 60, but with the addition of a small percentage of tin (making bronze) this rises to 140, and after hammering to 250. It is therefore not surprising that the widespread use of metals and the decline of flint tools and weapons began only during the 'Bronze Age', in the 2nd millennium BC.

Copper metallurgy may not have impinged noticeably upon the life of the average peasant before 2000 BC, but it nevertheless had a broad social and economic significance. As may be imagined, it was a highly skilled craft which took centuries to evolve. Its growth went hand in hand with the development of craft specialization and primitive chiefdoms, outlined above. Chiefs were needed to organize and allocate the specialized work of the craftsmen; they were also needed to redistribute the 'wealth' that the new crafts generated. Of course the chiefs themselves would have wished to show their rank and authority by making a public display of their own great wealth. What better way to do this than by showing off objects made of the new but scarce mineral, copper? In real life they would have paraded copper axes and trinkets during ceremonies; in death — where the archaeologist can observe them — they displayed this wealth to the gods in the form of rich burials.

Although there are a number of rich graves in the late 'Copper Age' of, for instance, the Carpathian basin, the emphasis upon status and rank in burials only became marked in the Bronze Age of the 2nd millennium BC, when what we might call a true 'warrior aristocracy' appeared. The proximity of the people of the middle Danube and central Europe to the rich copper ores of the Carpathians and eastern Alps, and to the scarce tin deposits of southern Bohemia, made this area the power-house of social and economic development from the Bronze Age to the Early Iron Age. In this great region the increasing emphasis upon wealth, and the growing size and complexity of communities, is reflected in the ever larger and more elaborate burials that are found.

Along the middle Danube communal cemeteries for the dead, only introduced in the 3rd millennium BC, expanded in size from some 150 burials in the late 3rd millennium to an average of 1000 burials by the late 2nd millennium. During the height of the Bronze Age, members of the warrior élite began to be buried under specially constructed mounds or tumuli. Čaka, in south-west Slovakia, is one of the most famous. Here a chief was cremated and entombed under a mound 5 metres high, together with the earliest known bronze armour — embossed helmet and breastplate — swords, spears, axes, chisels, razors, fibulae, pins, belt-rings and seven fluted, graphite-polished pots. Slightly later an even wealthier warrior was cremated in a royal barrow at Očkov, also in Slovakia. Here the chief was dressed at his death in full regal regalia, including over 144 bronze weapons and ornaments, and buried beneath a huge funerary pyre of ash, bones and pottery.

The trend continued into the Iron Age. Iron metallurgy spread to Europe from Anatolia early in the 1st millennium BC. The much more widespread availability of the iron ores brought metals to the masses in the shape of farm tools and implements. Even so the gap between rich and poor continued to widen. Chiefs' burials were now even more fantastic

affairs. At Býčí Skála in Moravia, for instance, a cave close to some iron workings was excavated in the 19th century. In it were found the remains of great royal funeral pyres of the 6th century BC, containing fragments of four-wheeled wagons, harness fittings, bronze vessels, jewellery and pottery. Clearly a drunken funerary feast had been held at which some forty attendants, mostly women, had been sacrificed to honour the dead king, together with horses and other animals.

The growing complexity of burial rites in Bronze and Early Iron Age central Europe is reflected in every other aspect of society. Chiefs became more and more powerful as the need for better organization increased. Mining and metallurgy became more specialized. Mines in the Mühlbach-Bischofshofen district of Austria had a large permanent labour force, which produced ores not only for regions near at hand but also for export to far off Holland and Scandinavia, where no local ores existed. Farming became more intensified to feed the growing populations. Villages expanded, but were now sited as

Stonehenge—a cult monument to set beside the pyramids. Many of the stones used in its construction were brought from the Prescelly mountains in Pembrokeshire, 132 miles away. Recent research has shown that the uprights may well have been aligned for the purpose of making astronomical observations.

Overleaf: *A typical fortified village at the beginning of the Iron Age in Europe, about 1000 BC.*

One such warrior élite we can in fact name, thanks to the advance of literate civilizations from the south. These are the Celts. Their homeland seems to have been that area of east-central Europe which saw the greatest flowering of the Bronze Age. But the pressures of growing population and the mobility given by the horse seem to have stimulated an expansion westwards around 500 BC. Celtic culture spread right across Europe to France and eventually Britain, giving rise to a unique art style. Celtic art is largely non-naturalistic, portraying people and animals only in stylized forms, on bronze, silver or gold weapons and ornaments. Its influence was so profound that some of its traditions lingered on into the lst century AD and beyond, when civilization and literacy had been brought to much of Europe by the Romans.

This is how the story of the birth of civilization in Europe usually ends. Ultimately, it is said, civilization came from the south and east; it was not an indigenous development. But if we may be allowed to measure the degree of 'civilization' of a society by its achievements, perhaps we should set beside the towns and temples of Mesopotamia and the pyramids of Egypt a monument created by the illiterate inhabitants of 3rd- and 2nd-millennium Britain: Stonehenge. Begun by Neolithic farmers and completed by a Bronze Age warrior élite, Stonehenge stands as a unique testament to the skills of a society without benefit of 'civilization' as traditionally defined — writing, cities, roads. It serves to remind us that although we tend to see man's progress from ape-man to cultured human being as culminating in the great civilizations of the Near East, China, India, and the Americas, a high point of human creativity may be reached at any moment in history and anywhere in the world — from the Palaeolithic cave paintings of southern France to the monumental stone sculptures of prehistoric Polynesia.

much for defence as for proximity to good agricultural land. The great site of Wittnauer Horn near the Swiss-German border had a spectacular position, perched on a promontory 100 m above the surrounding land. Within its stone-and-earth rampart lay some seventy rectangular dwellings, huddled together for security. Warfare became endemic, as land grew scarce and warriors, now mounted on horses tamed from the Eurasian steppe and armed with the frightening new slashing sword, roamed the plains.

219

A bird's-eye view of prehistory

	dates/geology	palaeontology	anthropology		duration	ages
Cenozoic	12 million years ago Pliocene	Tertiary flora and fauna, mammals, primates, particularly anthropoids		*Ramapithecus wickeri*	14 — 10 million	
				Australopithecus africanus	5 — 1 million	
Quaternary	2 million years ago Lower Pleistocene	mastodon, rhinoceros, large predators		*Homo habilis*	3 — 1 million	Old Stone Age or Lower Palaeolithic
				Homo erectus modjokertensis	2 — 1 million 500,000	
	400,000 years ago Middle Pleistocene	mammoth, primitive elephant, woolly rhinoceros, giant elk		*Homo erectus pekinensis*	500,000 300,000	
				Homo sapiens steinheimensis	200,000 40,000	Middle Old Stone Age or Middle Palaeolithic
	100,000 years ago Upper Pleistocene	elephant, bison, horse, deer, reindeer, aurochs, cave bear		*Homo sapiens neanderthalensis*	100,000 35,000	
					40,000	Stone Age Late Old or Upper Palaeolithic
				Homo sapiens sapiens	10,000	Mesolithic
	10,000 years ago Holocene or Recent	horse, bison, reindeer, deer, aurochs			8,000	Neolithic
				Homo sapiens sapiens	3,000	Bronze Age
					1,000	Protohistory
						History

industries	tools	discoveries and inventions
Osteodontokeratic? (bone, tooth and horn)		use of bones, horns and teeth as tools
'Pre-Chellean' 'Abbevillean'		oldest known stone tools made by man 900,000 years, hand-axes
Acheulian		500,000 years, discovery and use of fire
Clactonian		400,000 years, first sizeable hunting bands
Levalloisian		120,000 years, production of flake tools and weapons 80,000 years, mammoth hunting 60,000 years, ritual burials
Mousterian		
Aurignacian Solutrean Magdalenian		30,000 years, earliest bone carvings, cave paintings and drawings
Azilian Sauveterrean		12,000 years, invention of the bow 10,000 years, beginning of fishing, domestication of the dog
Tardenoisian ceramic		8,000 years, beginning of agriculture, cultivation of barley and wheat, first pottery
bronze		3,000 years, first monumental building in stone 3,000 — 1,000 years, use of copper, bronze and iron
iron		beginnings of civilization

Dating the finds

There are two main methods of dating fossil remains. One is the method of **relative** dating, by which a specimen can be dated as contemporary with, or earlier or later than, another specimen or geological deposit. The other method is **absolute** dating, in which the specimen, or the deposit that contains it, can be dated in actual years before the present (b.p.). The latter method has been possible only in the last thirty years, with the advent of dating techniques based on radioactive decay, such as the radiocarbon, potassium-argon and uranium-thorium methods. Each has its own limitations in terms of the materials required and the range of ages which can be measured. For example, the radiocarbon technique is limited to dating organic material less than 70,000 years old, whereas the potassium-argon method requires volcanic rocks which are older than that date.

But the majority of hominid fossils can be dated only relatively, and it is necessary to discuss briefly the means by which they are assigned an age. The Quaternary period (in which we are living) consists of the Pleistocene (which began about two million years ago) and the Holocene or Recent (which began about 12,000 years ago). The subdivisions of the Pleistocene (Upper, Middle and Lower) have been defined by changes in the animals and plants recorded in rocks from both marine and land sequences. One of the defining characteristics of the Pleistocene is the series of climatic swings which resulted in the spread of ice-sheets over the northern continents of the world. These climatic changes profoundly affected the animals and plants of the temperate zones: during the colder stages animals such as the reindeer, woolly mammoth and woolly rhinoceros thrived in the periglacial 'tundra' environments of Europe, displacing such animals as the hippopotamus and the straight-tusked elephant which were adapted to warmer conditions. Such changes, and the relative evolution of the animals themselves through time, helped in the correlation of deposits, and this helped to establish a sequence of ice ages, to which fossil hominids and artefacts could be related. The ice advanced and retreated at about the same times in Europe and North America, but the ice ages, and the warmer interglacial periods, have been given different names in Europe, the Alps, the USA and Britain. A table will make things clearer.

Temperature curve (deep-sea cores)	Years ago	Mammal stages	Local glacial/interglacial sequences				Cultural events	Fossil men
			Alpine	European	N. American	British		
cold warm	10,000	HOLOCENE or RECENT				Flandrian	Use of metals, agriculture etc.	
	50,000	UPPER PLEISTOCENE	Würm	Weichsel	Wisconsin	Devensian	Upper Palaeolithic	Cro-Magnons
	100,000		Riss-Würm	Eem	Sangamon	Ipswichian	Mousterian or Middle Palaeolithic	Neanderthals
	150,000	MIDDLE PLEISTOCENE	Riss	Saale		Wolstonian		
	200,000							
	250,000		Mindel-Riss	Holstein	Illinois?	Hoxnian	Swanscombe hand-axe stage	
	300,000		Mindel?	Elster?		Anglian?		early *Homo sapiens*
	350,000		increasing	Cromerian complex?	Yarmouth?	late Cromerian?	Earliest tools in Britain?	
	400,000		uncertainty of					
	450,000		sequences					
	500,000							
	1,000,000	LOWER PLEISTOCENE	Gunz?		Kansas?		First hand-axes appear in Africa	*Homo erectus*
	2,000,000							*Homo habilis*
increasing fluctuations in climate		PLIOCENE					Oldowan pebble tools	*Australopithecus*
							Use of metals, agriculture etc.	

One problem in correlating these deposits is that the Alpine glaciers were never directly linked with the northern European ice-sheets, which originated from Scandinavia and may have developed independently. It is also difficult to find complete sequences and to obtain absolute dates for the various events, since Europe suffered little volcanic activity during the Pleistocene and volcanic deposits are a necessity for potassium-argon dating. However, recent studies of deep-sea cores and palaeomagnetism have provided the means by which the land sequences may eventually be correlated. The study of changes in the chemical and biological composition of long sequences of drillings from the sea bed has built up a picture of temperature changes in the sea which can be compared with the land sequence of ice-sheet advances and retreats. The most complete of the deep-sea cores (with events dated by the uranium-thorium technique) suggest that warm and cold stages occurred about every 100,000 years during the later Pleistocene, but in detail the cycles were quite complex.

The Earth's climate during the Pleistocene seems to have been controlled by three independent factors connected with the Earth's orbit and its orientation towards the sun. These three factors working in concert plunged the Earth into an ice age or a period of warmth, but working in opposition they produced a complicated series of climatic swings.

So the Alpine and North European schemes of glaciations are certainly an oversimplification, and it is only in the last 200,000 years (covering the Upper Pleistocene) that the deep-sea core record correlates well with the record of land deposits.

The technique of palaeomagnetism has a more direct relevance to land deposits since the Earth's magnetic field is unstable and periodically reverses itself or changes its orientation. Rocks can pick up the prevailing magnetic orientation at the time of their deposition and hence can be dated relatively to each other if a good sequence is known. Again, the complete picture for the Pleistocene is a very complex one of many reversals and returns to a 'normal' polarity (i.e. like that of today). However, the evidence of palaeomagnetism has shown that early 'Cromerian' deposits in Europe contain a return to a normal polarity which is already dated from outside Europe at 700,000 years ago. This provides a reasonable date for early Middle Pleistocene deposits in Europe and a maximum age for fossils such as the Heidelberg (Mauer) jaw. One additional method of relative dating is the use of artefacts associated with deposits and fossil hominids. The Palaeolithic or Old Stone Age began as early as the Pliocene (at least two million years ago) with the appearance of the first stone tools. The Lower Palaeolithic stage encompassed the pebble-tool industries and the hand-axe industries. The Middle Palaeolithic stage was, strictly speaking, confined to the areas of Europe, western Asia and North Africa. It is equivalent to the term 'Mousterian' and probably covered a time-span of less than 100,000 years, up to about 35,000 years ago. The Upper Palaeolithic, associated in Europe with the appearance of Cro-Magnon man, was characterized by the predominance of blade tools, a much greater use of bone, antler and ivory, and the first flowering of art. It lasted from about 35,000 to 12,000 years ago, ending with the end of the last Pleistocene cold stage.

Further reading

BODMER, W. F., and L. L. Cavalli-Sforza: *Genetics, Evolution and Man.* W. H. Freeman, Reading and San Francisco, 1976

BROTHWELL, D. R.: *The Rise of Man.* Sampson Low, Maidenhead, 1976

CAMPBELL, B. G.: *Human Evolution.* Aldine, Chicago, 1974

CLARK, W. E. Le Gros: *History of the Primates.* University of Chicago Press, 1966; British Museum (Natural History), London, 1970

DAY, M. H.: *Fossil Man.* Hamlyn, Feltham (Middlesex), 1974
— : *Guide to Fossil Man.* Cassell, London, 1977

DYER, K. F.: *The Biology of Racial Integration.* Scientechnica, Bristol, 1974

The Editors of *Time-Life* Books: *The Emergence of Man.* Time-Life International, New York, 1953. (This is the group title of a series of four books: *The Missing Link, The First Men, The Neanderthals,* and *Cro-Magnon Man.)*

GIBLETT, E.: *Genetic Markers in Human Blood.* Blackwell, Oxford, 1969; Lippincott, Philadelphia, 1969

HARRISON, G. A., and others: *Human Biology.* Oxford University Press, 1977

HIERNAUX, J.: *The People of Africa.* Weidenfeld & Nicolson, London, 1973; Scribner, New York, 1973

HOWELLS, W. W.: *Evolution of the Genus* Homo. Addison-Wesley, Reading (Mass.) and London, 1973
— : *The Pacific Islanders.* Weidenfeld & Nicolson, London, 1973

JOLLY, A.: *The Evolution of Primate Behaviour.* Macmillan, London and New York, 1972

KATZ, S. H. (introduction by): *Biological Anthropology. Readings from Scientific American.* W. H. Freeman, Reading and San Francisco, 1975

LEHMANN, H., and R. G. Huntsman: *Man's Haemoglobins including Haemoglobinopathy.* Elsevier, Amsterdam, 1974

MOURANT, A. E., and others: *The Distribution of the Human Blood Groups and Other Polymorphisms.* Oxford University Press, 1976

NAPIER, J. R.: *The Roots of Mankind.* Smithsonian, Washington, 1970; Allen & Unwin, London, 1971

NAPIER, P.: *Monkeys and Apes.* Hamlyn, Feltham (Middlesex), 1970; Bantam, New York, 1973

NAPIER, J. R. and P.: *Handbook of Living Primates.* Academic Press, New York and London, 1967

OAKLEY, K. P.: *Man the Toolmaker.* British Museum (Natural History), London, 1972

PILBEAM, D.: *The Ascent of Man.* Macmillan, London and New York, 1972

ROMER, A. S.: *Vertebrate Paleontology.* University of Chicago Press 1966

ROSEN, S. I.: *Introduction to the Primates.* Prentice-Hall, Englewood Cliffs, N. J., 1974

SIMONS, E. L.: *Primate Evolution.* Macmillan, London and New York, 1972

STEWART, T. D.: *The People of America.* Weidenfeld & Nicolson, London, 1973; Scribner, New York, 1973

TATTERSALL, I.: *Man's Ancestors.* John Murray, London, 1970; Transatlantic, Levittown, N. Y., 1971

WEINER, J. S.: *Man's Natural History.* Weidenfeld & Nicolson, London, 1971; Doubleday, New York, 1973 (under the title *The Natural History of Man)*

WOOD, B.: *The Evolution of Early Man.* Peter Lowe, London, 1976

YOUNG, J. Z.: *Introduction to the Study of Man.* Oxford University Press, 1974

Index

Page numbers in italics refer to illustrations

— *rhodesiensis* 80, 85—89
— *sapiens* 7, 10, 11, 13, 24, 85, 101, *103*, 105, *124, 125*, 157, 183
— *soloensis* 80
horse 23, 113, *123*, 134, *140*, 143, 161, 183, 184, 185, *208*, 218, 219
Hottentots *168*, 171, 173
houses and huts 75, 79, *116*, 130, 134, 184, 186, *188*, 198, 202, *207*, 208, 212, 217
howler monkeys 28
Hungary 35, 60, 161, 208
hunter-fishermen 116—18, *192*, 194, 204, 205, 212
hunter-gatherers 55, 59, 105, 113—20, *121*, 158, 165, 166, 171, 174, 184, *186*, 194, 198, 207
hunting 35, 50, 58, 68—69, *89, 92, 94, 97, 109, 111, 113, 121, 123*, 157, 159, 165, 168, 174, 179, 184—86
huts, *see* houses
Hylobates 31
Hylobatidae 30

ibex *90*, 97, *123*
ice ages 77, 125, 129, 157, 158—59, 174, 184, 188; Saale (Wolstonian, Illinois, Riss) 76
ice sheets, advance and retreat of 55, 105, 113, 125, 158, 162, 174, 183, 184—85, 186, 193
Ichthyornis 22
Ichthyostega 20
igloo 119, 179
incest taboo 138
India 7, 31, 35, 160, 161, 162, 219
Indians, American *12*, 116, 160, 174—79
Indonesia 157, 158, 160, 161, 168
inheritance 198—201
interglacial periods 24, 75, 76; Holstein (Hoxnian, Yarmouth, Mindel-Riss) 75
Iran 183, 196, 201, 212
iron 14, 173, 217—18; pyrites 126
Iron Age 171, 173, 183, 217—18
irrigation 183, 204, 212, 215—16
Italy 76, 78, 207—08
ivory 13, 120, 123, 125, 129, 130, 134, 143

Java 12, 30, 55, 56—58, *61*, 67, 80, 85, 162, 165
Java man *55*, 57
Jericho 202
jewellery and ornaments 108, 129, 202, 208, 216, 218
Jurassic 21—22

Kabwe, Zambia 85, 100
kayak 119, 179
Kenya 28, 35, 39, 55, 57, 65, 89, *173*
Khants 118
Khoisan peoples 171, 173

kitchen middens 193, 194
Klasies Cave, S. Africa 100
knives 12, 14, 123, 126, 129, 179, *186*, 202
knives, reaping (sickles) 14, 186, *188*
knuckle-walking 32
Köln-Lindenthal, W. Germany 208
Koobi Fora, Kenya 57, 65
Kostienki, U.S.S.R. 131, 134
Krapina, Yugoslavia *86*, 92, 97
Kromdraai, Transvaal 38, 44
Krzemionki, Poland 216
Kudaro, U.S.S.R. 92

La Chapelle, France 92
Laetolil, Tanzania 48
La Ferrassie, France 92
lampshells 18
Lamuts 119
La Naulette, Belgium 92
language 11, 75, 105, 162, 168, 173, 179
    Aryan 162
    Bantu 171, 173
    Dravidian group 162
Lapland 113; Lapps 119
Lascaux cave, France 105, 125, *140, 144*
Lazaret, France 78
Leakey, L.S.B. *27*, 29, 39, 49
Leakey, Richard 81
leg 10, 42, 49, 98, 165, 174
Le Moustier, France 13, 89, 92, *98*
lemurs 7, 8, 27
Leroi-Gourhan, A. 151
Les Trois-Frères cave, France 144
life, origins of 17
lighting 119
Limnopithecus 29
Lion Hill cave, China 80
literacy 219; *see also* writing
llama 194, *196*, 215
lorises 7, 8, 27
Los Angeles man 174
lung-fishes 19

Magdalenian industry 125, 184, 186, 188
magic and magicians *135*, 140, 143—51
Maglemosians 188—93, 194
maize 215
Makapansgat, S. Africa 38, 44, 89
Malarnaud, France 92
Malaysia 7, 31, 168
mammals, primitive 20, 22—23
mammoth 24, *77, 109, 111*, 113, 129, 134, *140*, 143, 183, 184, 185; ivory 13, 129, *137, 143*
man: adaptation in 60, 98, 119, 120, 131, 159, 162, 165, 173, 174, 183, 186, 193, 204, 208; classification in nature 7—8; control of the environment 7, 11—14, 69, 134, 173, 174, 179, 183—84, 194, 196—98, 202, 204, 208—12, 215—16; cultural evolution of 60, 143—53,

183—84, 202—19; definition of 55—56; differences from other animals 7, 8—11, *31, 35, 47*; physical diversification of 11; see also *Homo* spp.
Maoris *167*, 168—70
Marquesas Islands *166*, 168
mastodon 23
'*Maueranthropus*' 60
Mbuti pygmies *168*, 174
Mediterranean in the Neolithic 129, 171, 183, 186, 204—08
megaliths 212; *see also* Stonehenge
Meganeura 20
'*Meganthropus*' 57
Melanesia/ns 160, 161, 162, 165, 166—68
melanin 159
Mesolithic 14, 174, 188—94, 204, 205, 206, 208, 212
Mesopotamia 7, 212, 214, 219
Mesosaurus 21
Mesozoic *18*, 21—22
microliths 186, 188
Micronesians 160, 168
Middle East 13, 157, 160, 161
millstones 14, 193
mining and metallurgy 216—17, 218
Miocene *22*, 23—24, 28—30, 35—36, 42, 50
Mongoloids *158*, 160—61, 168, 174—79
monkeys 8, 23, 28, 30, 31, 32, 174, 194
Monte Circeo, Italy 97
Montespan, France 151
Montmaurin, France 75
mother goddess cult 202
Mousterian industry 13, 89—90, 98
Mühlbach-Bischofshofen, Austria 218
Mungo, Lake, Australia 105, 162
musical instruments 108, 130

Natufians 186—88, *196*, 198
Ndutu, Tanzania 85
Neanderthal man 13, 24, 57, *75*, 76, 77, 78, 80, *82, 85, 86*, 89—101, 105, 108—09, 112, 134, 157—58; competition with Cro-Magnons 125
Neander valley, Germany *103*
Necrolemur 27
needles 13, 108
Negrillos 171
negritos 7
Negroids 160, 161, 162, *165, 168*, 171—74
Neolithic 14, 158, 160, 162, 178, 183, 188, 196—212; Mediterranean 129, 171, 183, 204—08
Newfoundland 179
New Guinea, *see* Papua
New Zealand 168
Ngandong 58, 80
Niah cave, Borneo 100, 105, 157
Nilotes 171, 173, *174, 175*
North Sea 193